ACCENT CONTROL

By Ron Spagnardi

Design And Layout By Joe King

Published By
Modern Drummer Publications, Inc.
12 Old Bridge Road
Cedar Grove, NJ 07009 USA

Contents

Accents add color and dynamic variation to our drumming, and they're an extremely essential aspect of every drummer's technique.

Accent Control is a technical study that will help you 1) improve your ability to execute accents with varied stickings, 2) develop a greater level of stick control, 3) increase the fluency of your weaker hand, 4) further refine the balance between your right and left hands, 5) improve your endurance, and 6) stimulate solo ideas for application on the drumset.

Part 1 of *Accent Control* demonstrates the use of accents with 8th notes. **Part 2** presents accented triplet patterns. And **Part 3** deals with 16th-note accents. Each part begins with 128 one-bar patterns played with varied stickings. The one-bar patterns are expanded to eighteen two-bar patterns, twelve four-bar exercises, and four solos that use most of the patterns previously studied.

Each part also includes a section on roll accents using alternate sticking in one-bar, two-bar, four-bar, and solo formats.

GETTING THE MOST FROM THIS BOOK

Repeat all of the one- and two-bar patterns at least *ten times* each. The four-bar exercises should be repeated at least *five times* each. Be sure to master each exercise before proceeding to the next.

Practice using all of the recommended stickings. Some are more difficult than others and may feel awkward at first. They will become more natural with consistent practice.

Be sure to make a very noticeable distinction between accented and unaccented notes. Use a full stroke and a strong wrist snap for all accented notes, and a much lower stick level for unaccented notes. Moving from one stick level to another, combined with the varied stickings, is excellent practice for hand control and balance.

All of the roll accents should also be played strongly, with a much softer non-accent. Play all rolls using a closed, buzz-roll technique.

Practice slowly at first, gradually increasing speed as your facility with the material improves. Use a metronome or drum machine to gauge your progress.

All of the material should also be played in the following manner: 1) Add the bass drum to all accented notes with each sticking. 2) Play the accents as rimshots along with the bass drum. 3) Play all accented notes as flams. 4) Move all accented notes around the drums with alternate sticking. Play non-accents on the snare drum, right-hand accents on the large tom-tom, and left-hand accents on the small tom-tom. Each approach is explained in greater detail on the first page of every part.

Take your time with each approach. Master each one through diligent practice, and you'll soon notice a marked improvement in your accenting ability and overall technique.

PART 1: 8TH-NOTE ACCENTS

All of the 8th-note accent patterns that follow use sticking variations a, b, c, and d shown below. The other examples demonstrate optional ways the patterns can be played. 1) Add the bass drum on all accents. 2) Play all accents as rimshots. 3) Play all accents as flams. 4) Play all accents using snare drum, small tom-tom, and large tom-tom. Practice all of the material in Part 1 using each of the methods described below.

ONE-BAR PATTERNS

In the following 128 one-bar exercises, stickings a and b use an alternating pattern, leading first with the right hand and then with the left. Sticking c uses double strokes, which can be quite challenging and excellent for bringing out the oftentimes weaker secondary stroke of the double-stroke roll. The paradiddle sticking presented in d is also beneficial for developing balance and control between the hands. Stickings c and d can be tough to master, so be prepared to spend additional practice time with both.

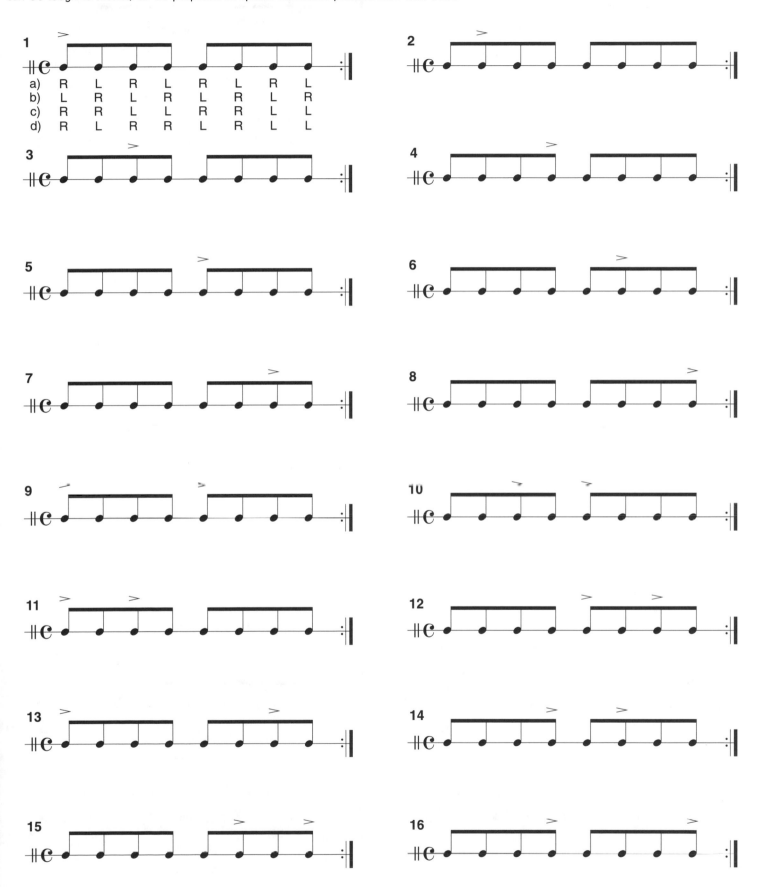

5

17

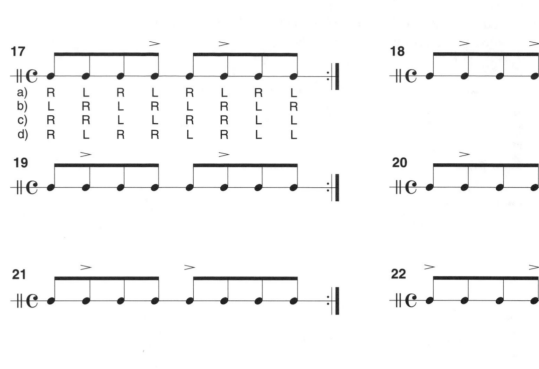

a)	R	L	R	L	R	L	R	L
b)	L	R	R	L	R	R	R	L
c)	R	R	L	R	L	R	L	L
d)	R	L	R	R	L	R	L	L

18

19

20

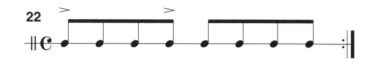

21

22

23

24

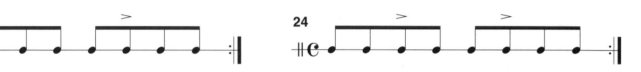

25

26

27

28

29

30

31

32

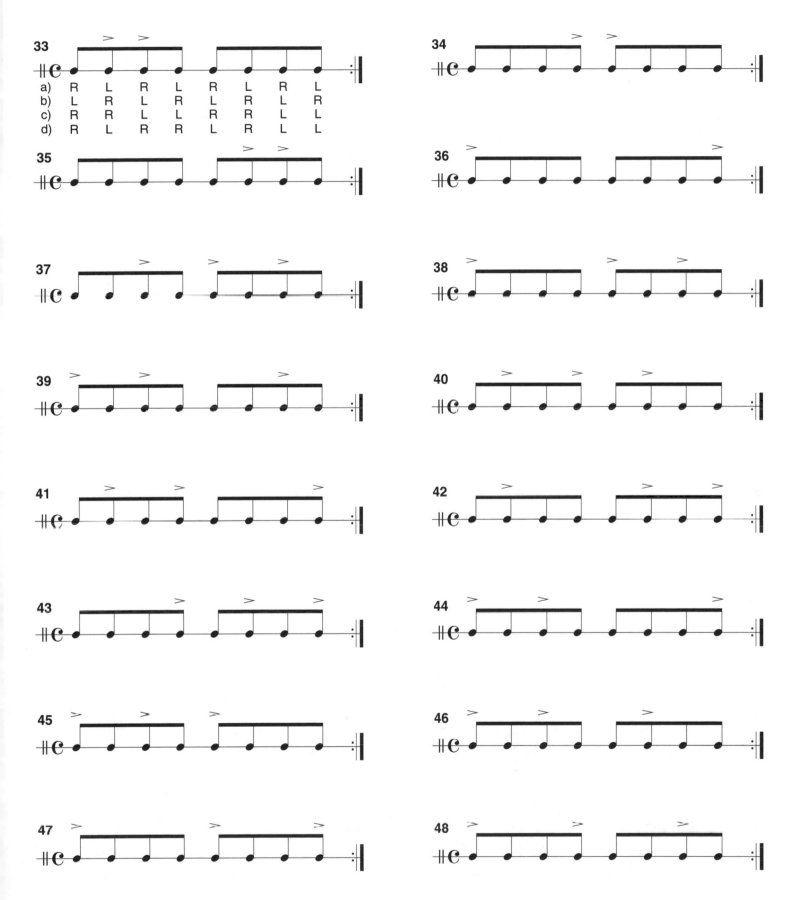

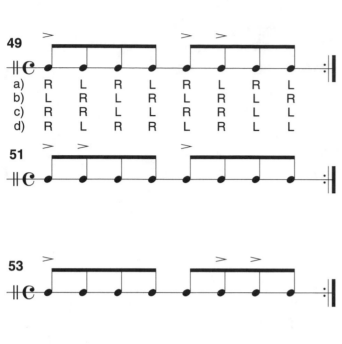

49

a) R L R L R L R L
b) L R R L R R L L
c) R R L L R R L L
d) R L R R L R L L

50

51

52

53

54

55

56

57

58

59

60

61

62

63

64

8

65

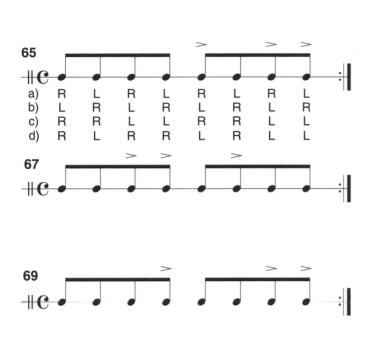

a) R L R L R L R L
b) L R R L R L L R L R L
c) R R L L R L R L L R L L
d) R L R R L R L L R L L

66

67

68

69

70

71

72

73

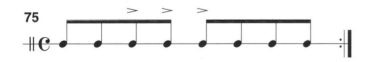

74

75

76

77

78

79

80

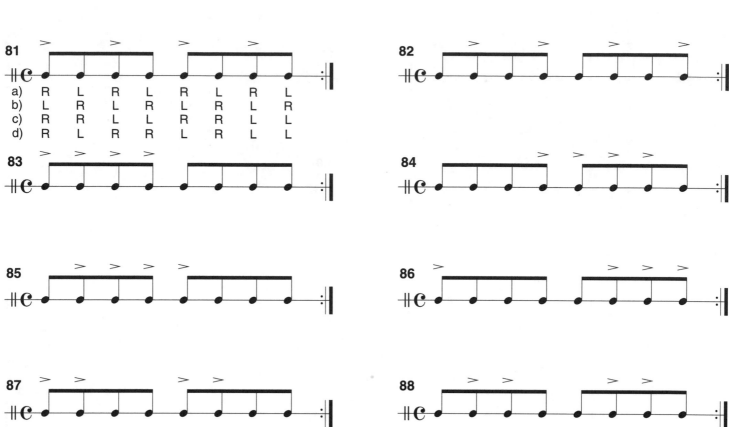

81
a) R L R L R L R L
b) L R R L L R R L
c) R R L L R R L L
d) R L R L R L R L

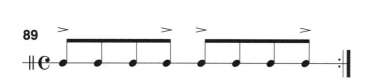
82

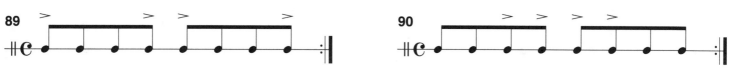
83 84

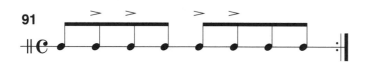
85 86

87 88

89 90

91 92

93 94

95 96

10

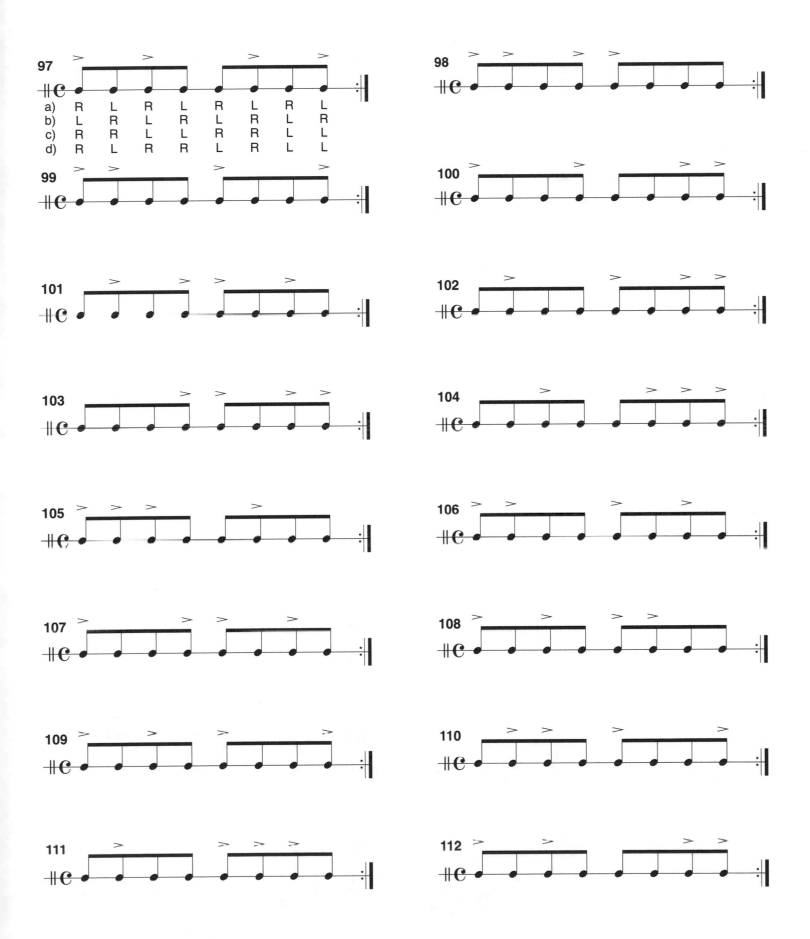

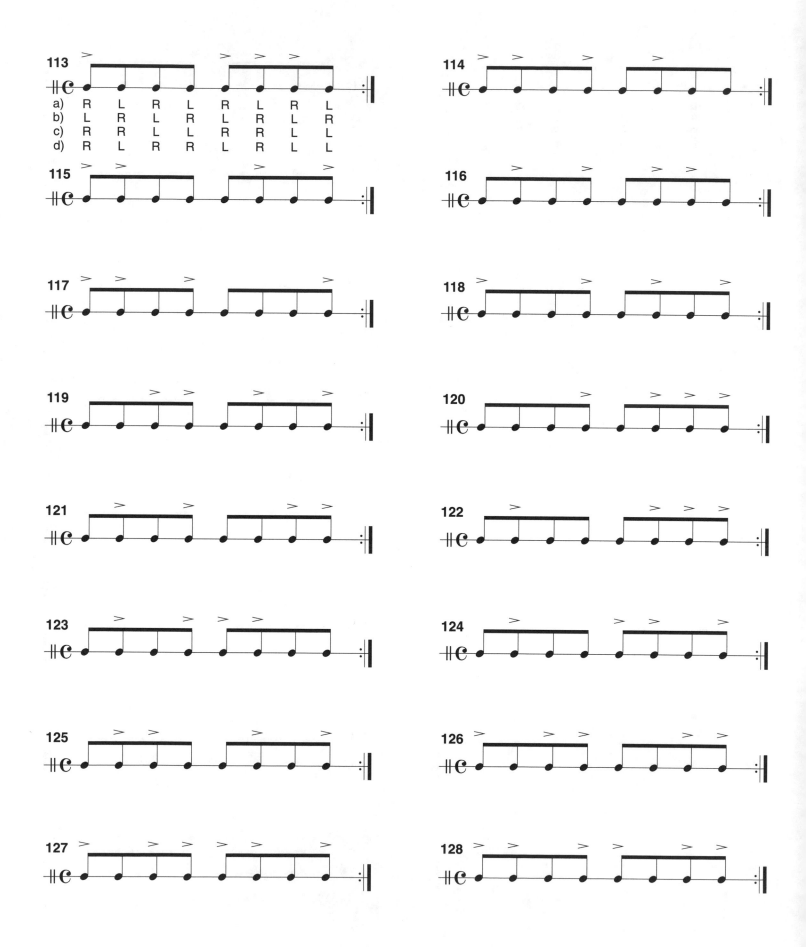

113
a) R L R L R L R L
b) L R L R L R L R
c) R R L L R R L L
d) R L R L R R L L

114

115

116

117

118

119

120

121

122

123

124

125

126

127

128

TWO-BAR PATTERNS

Practice these two-bar patterns in a similar manner to the one-bar exercises, using all of the varied methods described previously.

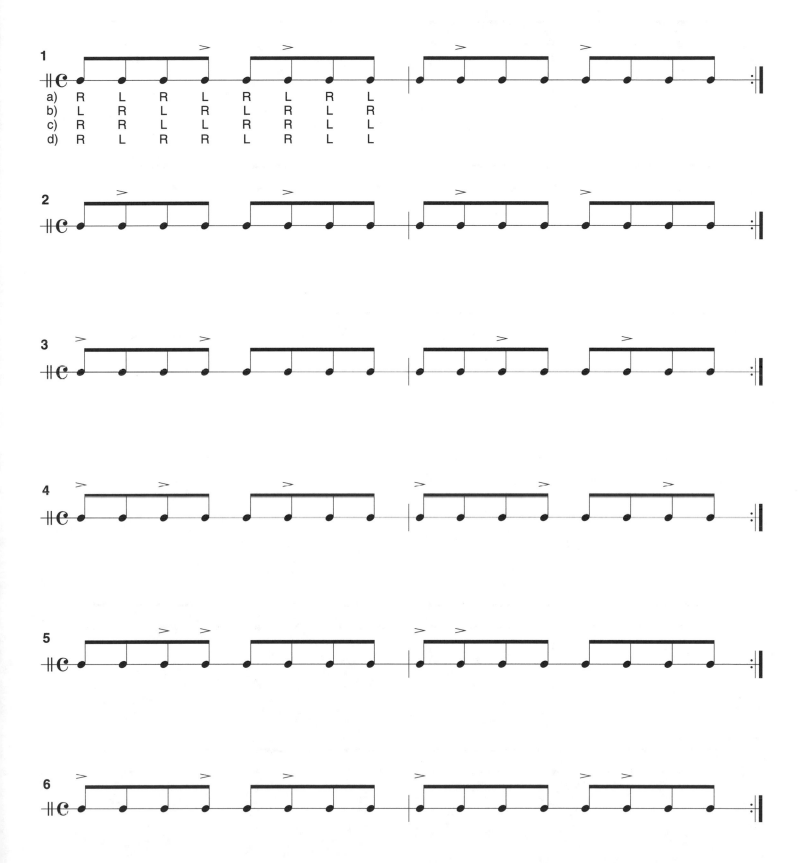

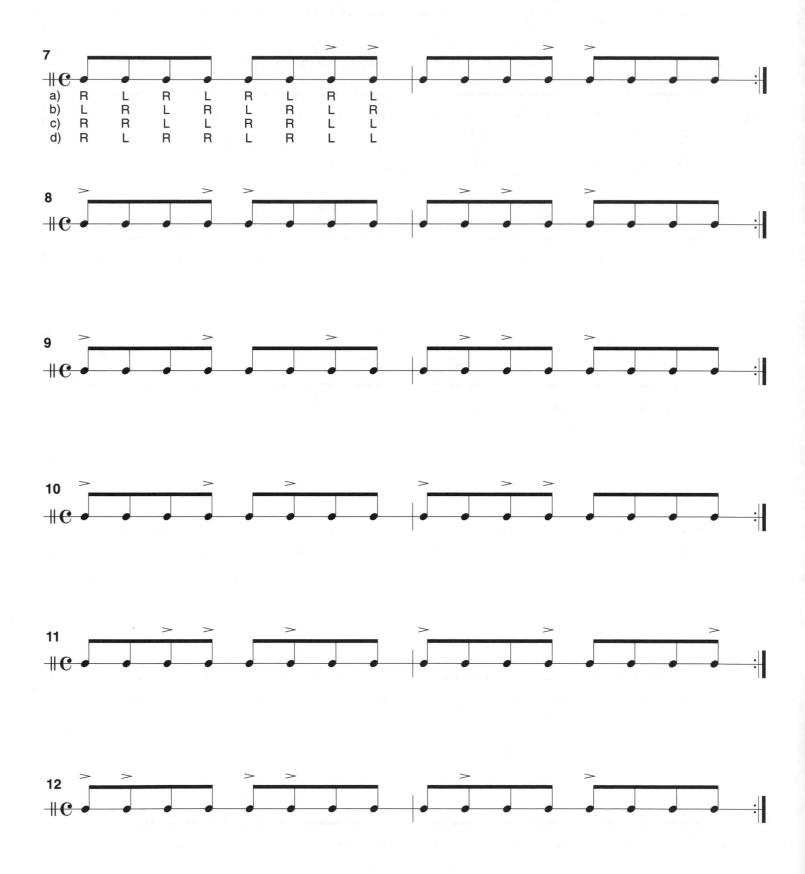

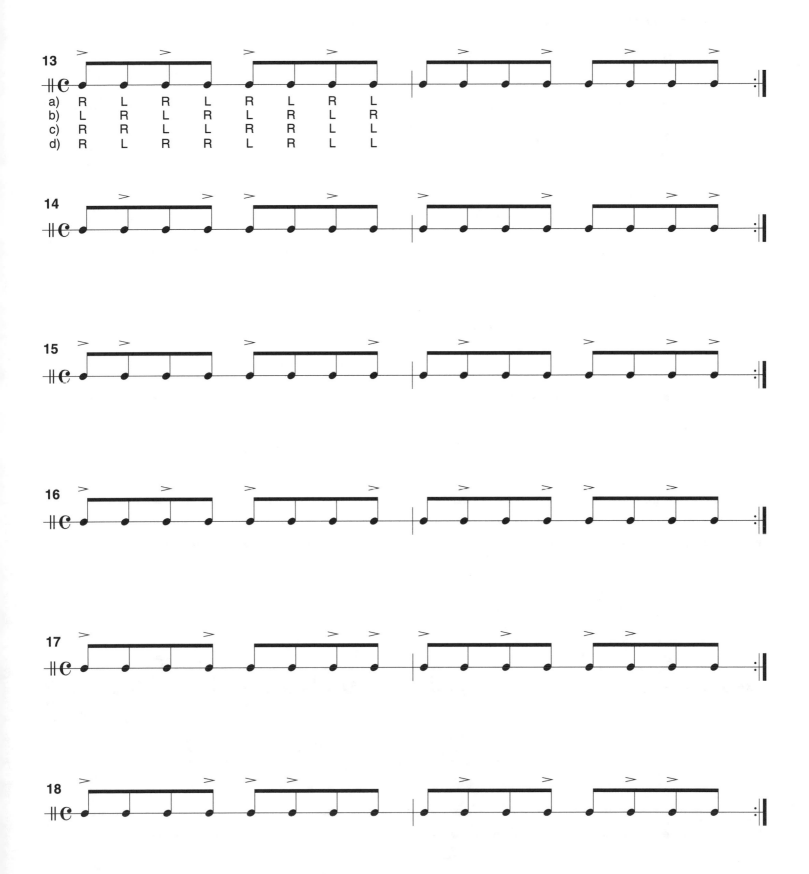

FOUR-BAR PATTERNS

Repeat each of these four-bar patterns at least five times before proceeding to the next one.

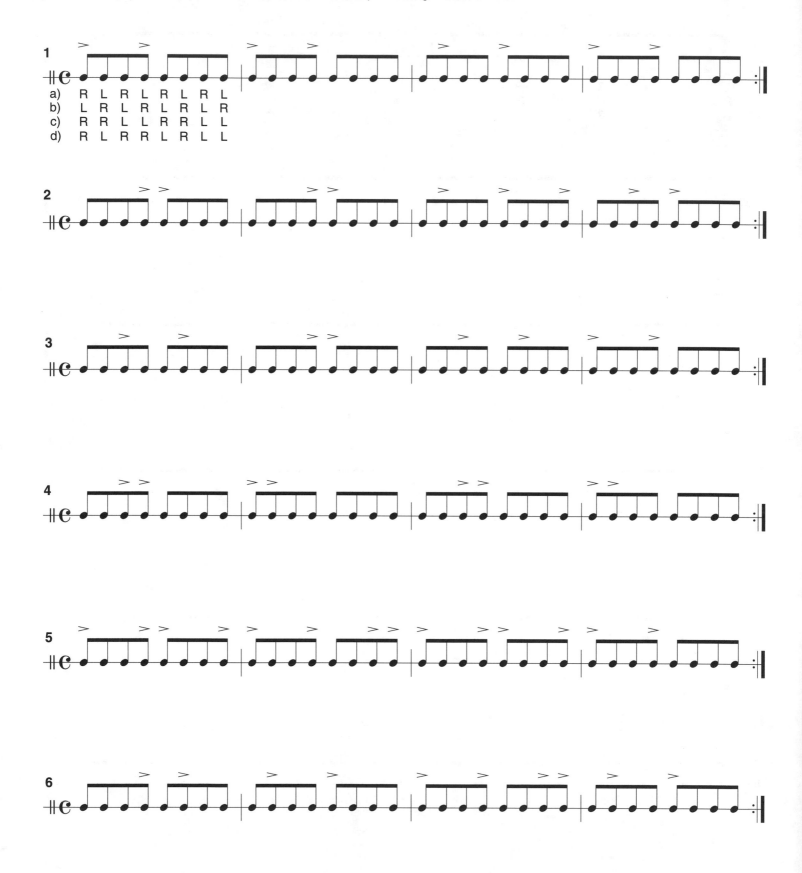

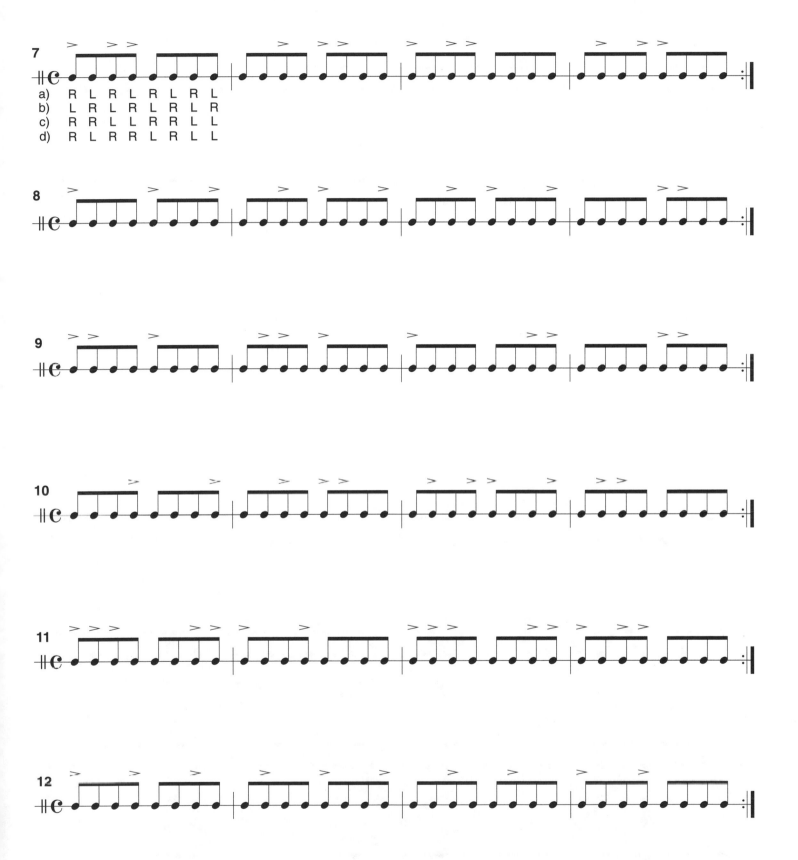

8TH-NOTE SOLO #1

This solo, and the three that follow, should be played using all four stickings. Then add the bass drum on all accented notes. Next, play all accents as rimshots with the bass drum, and then as alternating flams. Finally, using alternate sticking, practice the solos on the drums, playing unaccented notes on snare drum, right-hand accents on large tom-tom, and left-hand accents on the small tom-tom. Try these playing the bass drum in four, and then with the bass drum on all accented notes. See page 4 at the beginning of this section for a further description.

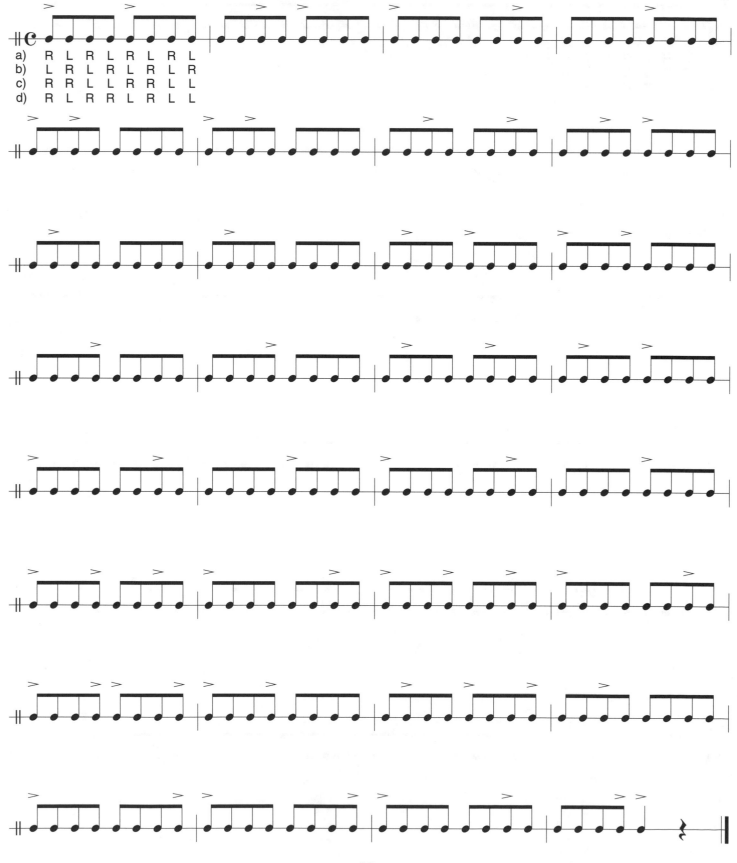

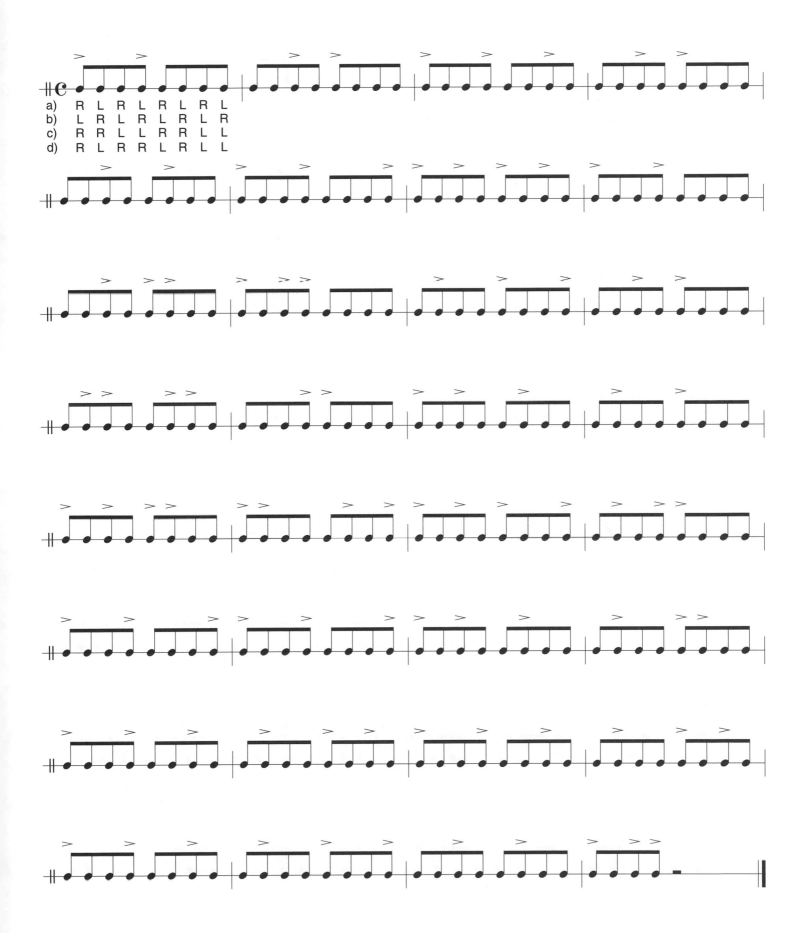

a) R L L R L R L R L
b) L R R L R L R L R
c) R R R L L R R L L
d) R L R R L R L L L

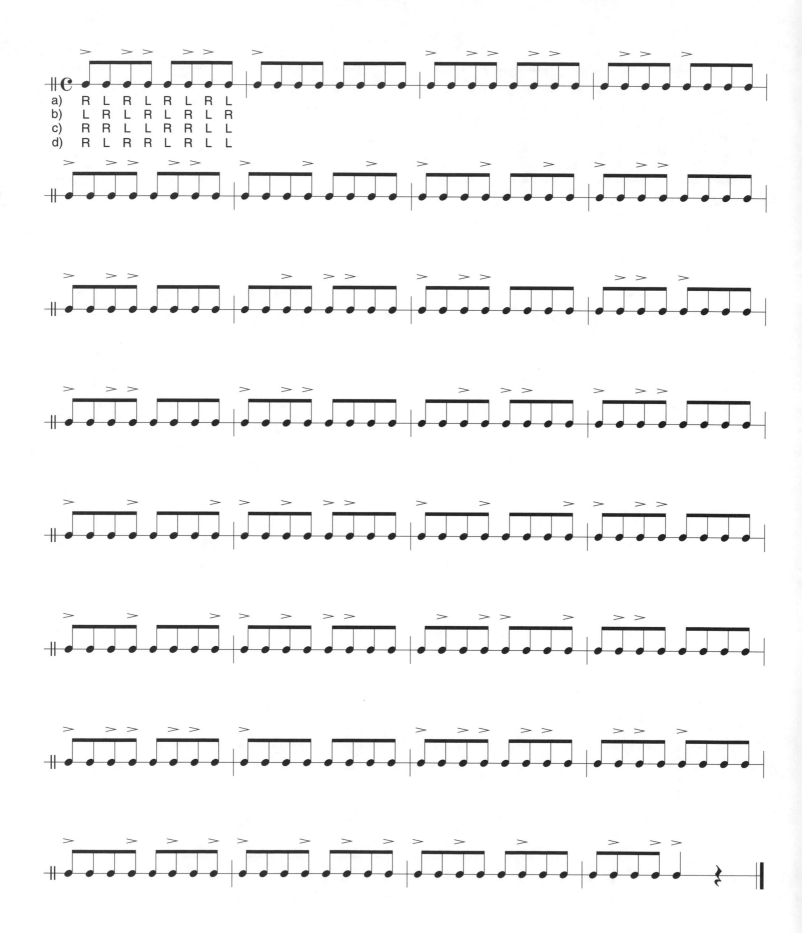

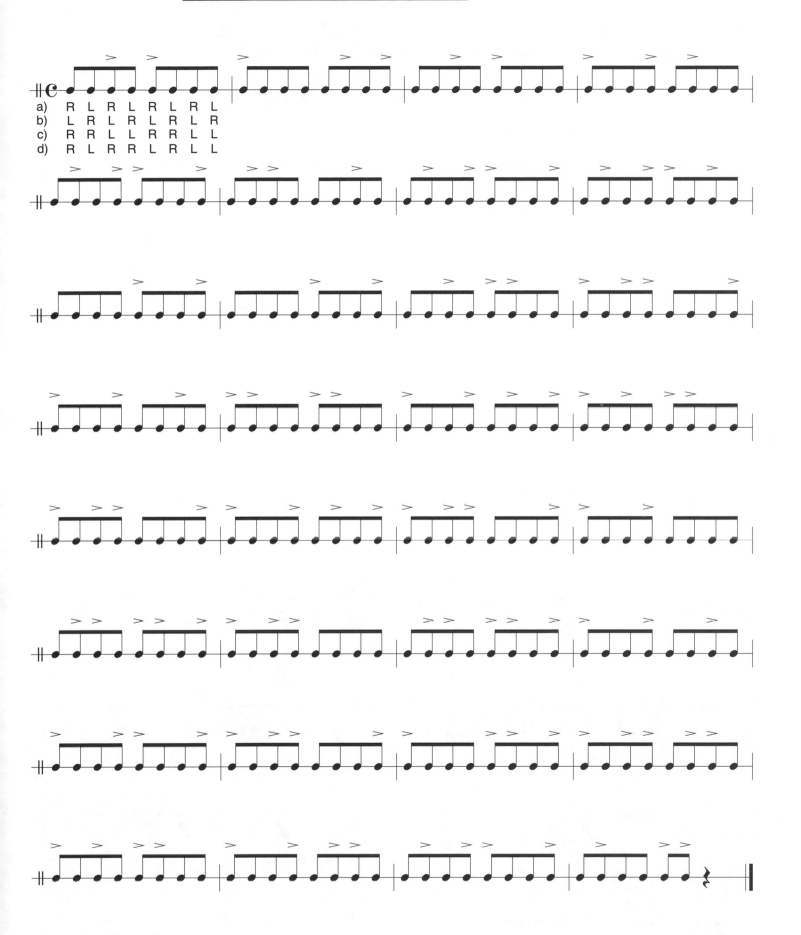

ONE-BAR ROLL PATTERNS

All of the following accented roll exercises should be played using a closed buzz roll. Be sure to play the accented notes stronger than the unaccented notes. These patterns should also be practiced with the bass drum on all accented notes as shown below.

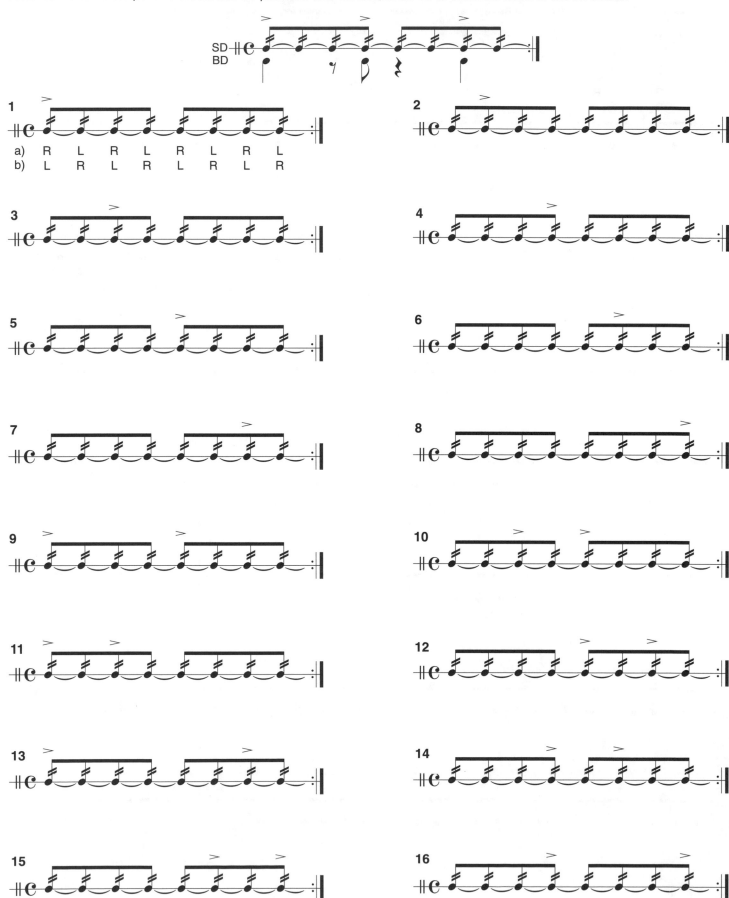

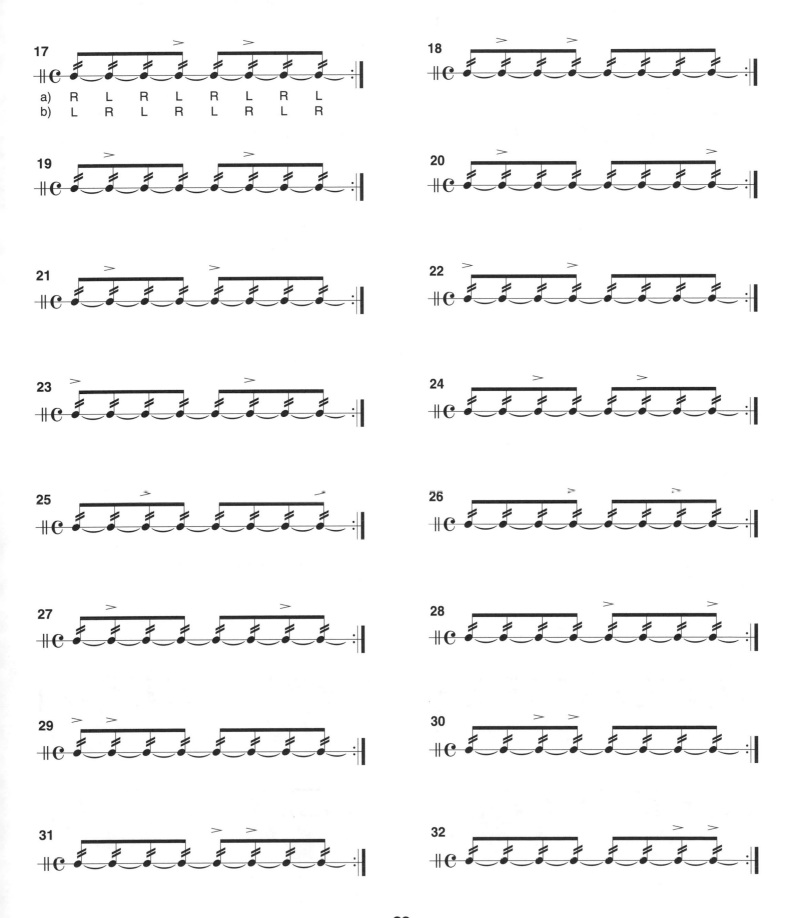

23

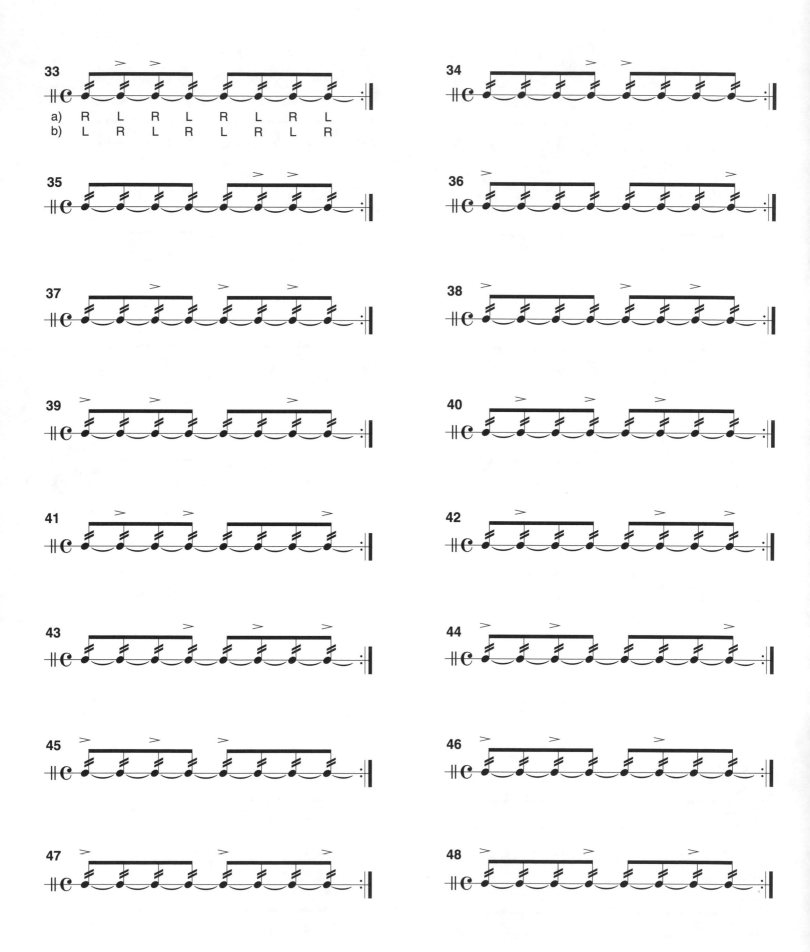

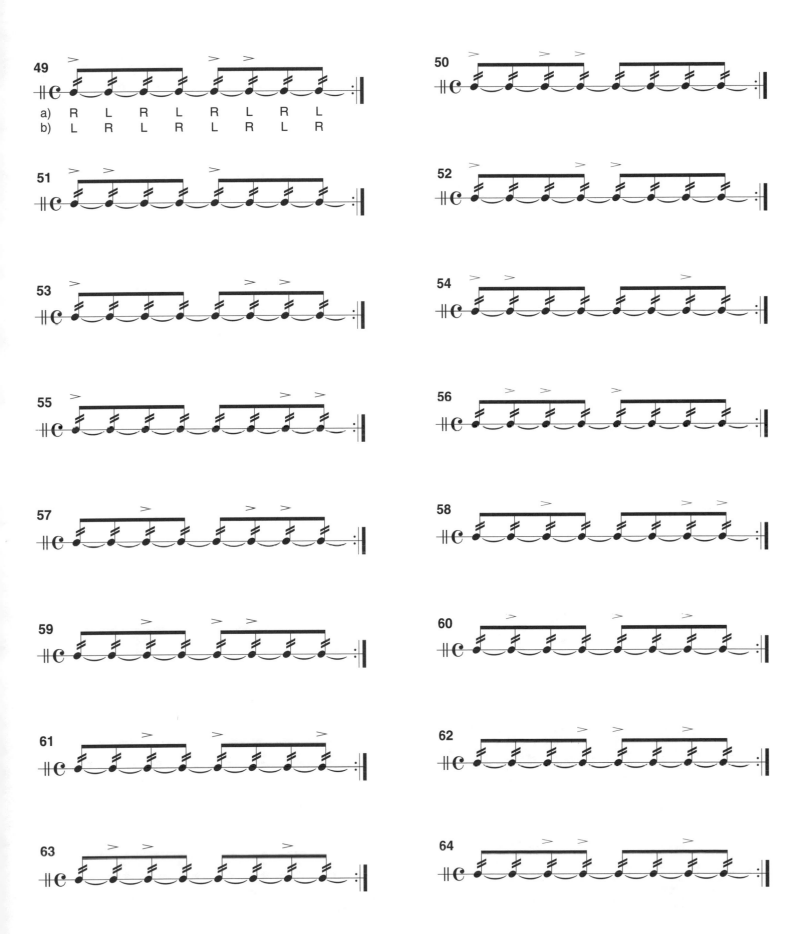

25

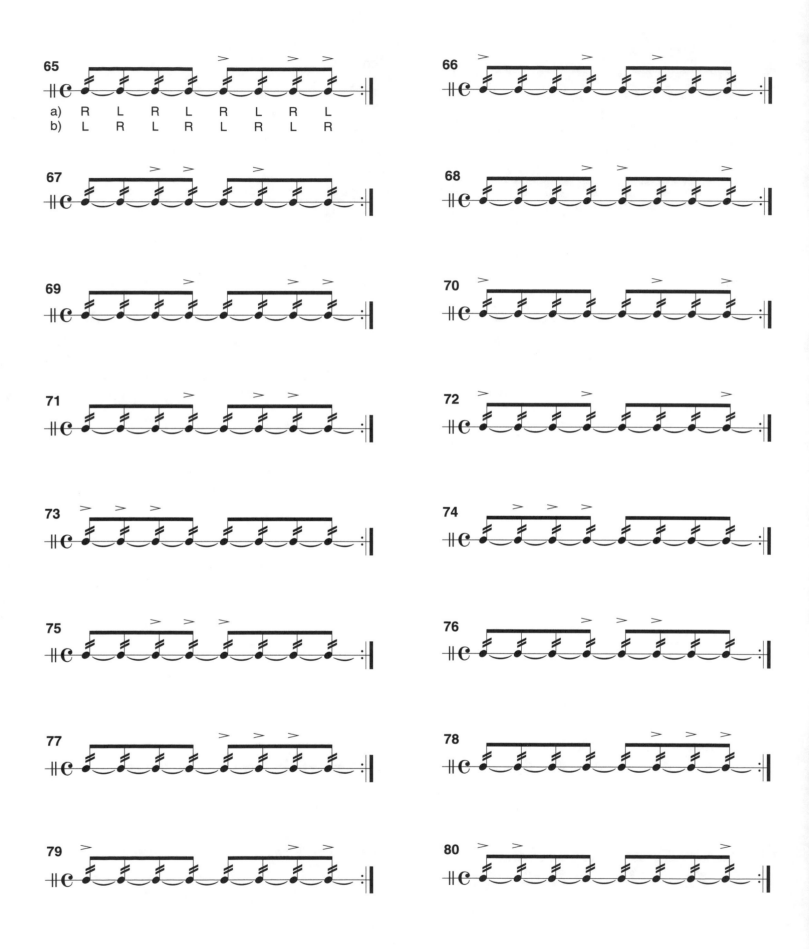

65
a) R L R L R L R L
b) L R L R L R L R

66

67

68

69

70

71

72

73

74

75

76

77

78

79

80

26

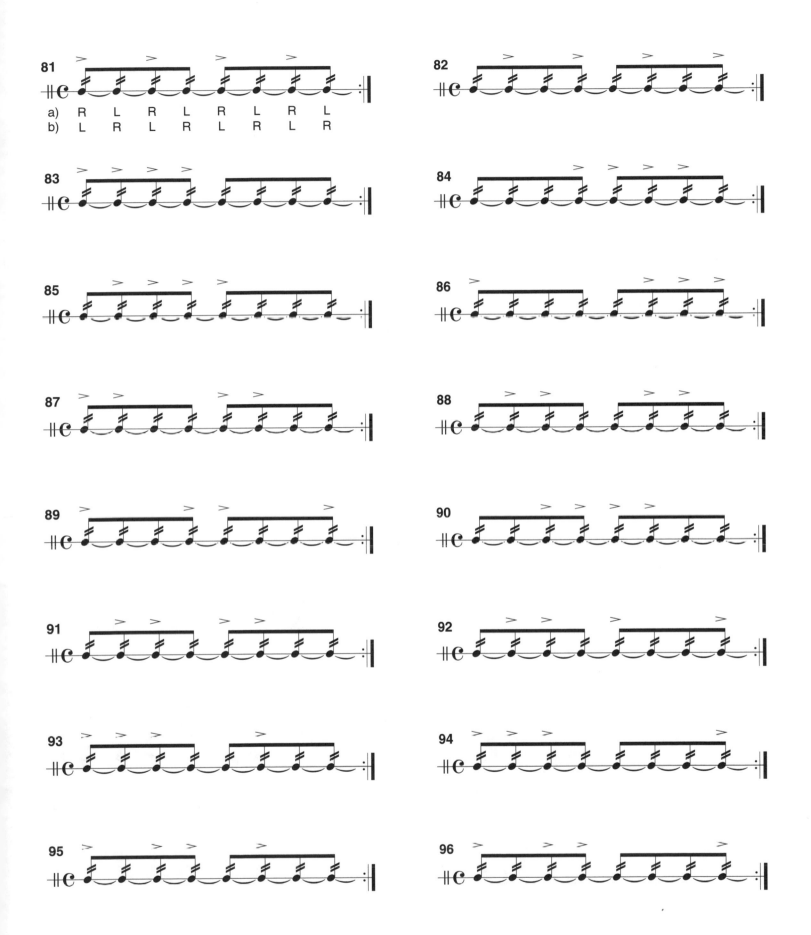

81
a) R L R L R L R L
b) L R L R L R L R

82

83

84

85

86

87

88

89

90

91

92

93

94

95

96

27

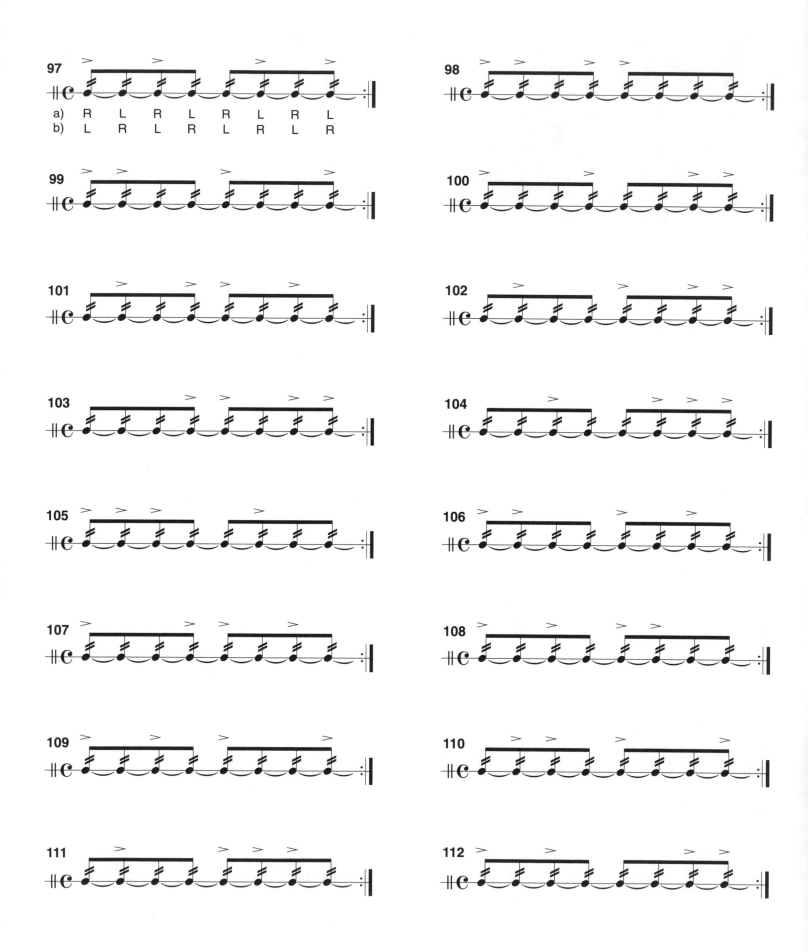

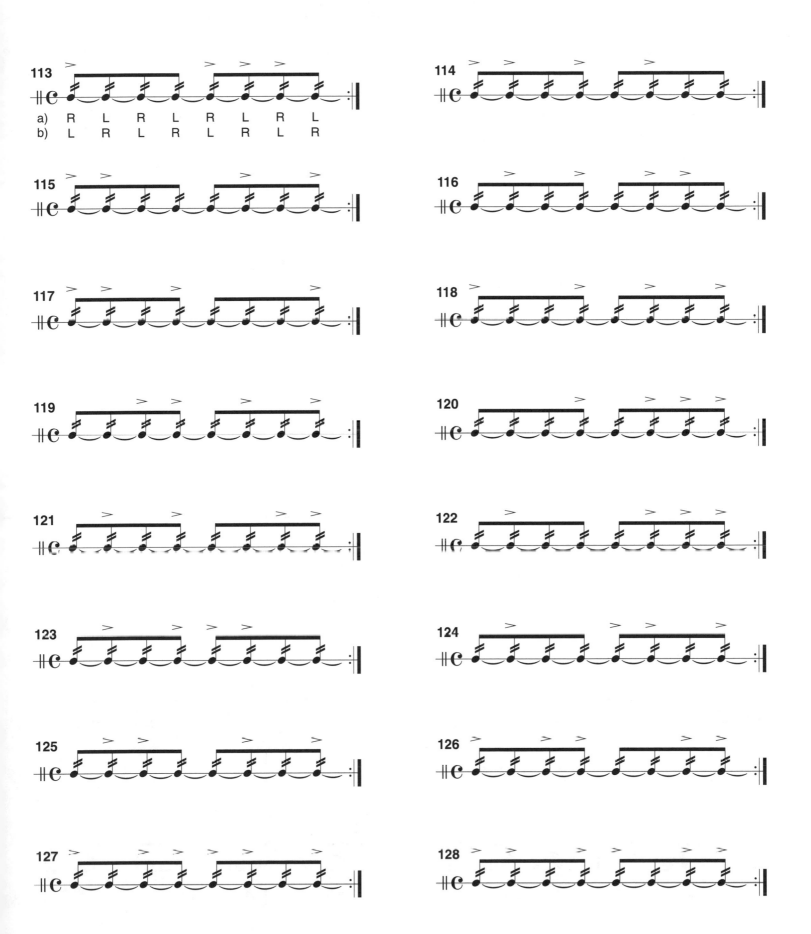

TWO-BAR ROLL PATTERNS

Take your time with these two-bar roll exercises. Increase speed gradually as your facility improves.

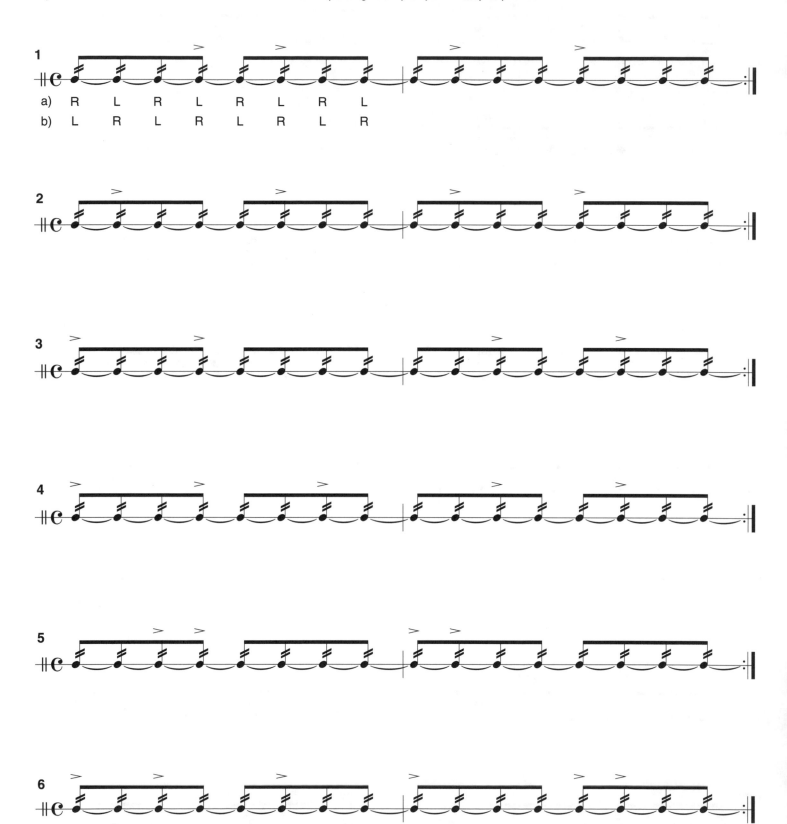

1
a) R L R L R L R L
b) L R L R L R L R

2

3

4

5

6

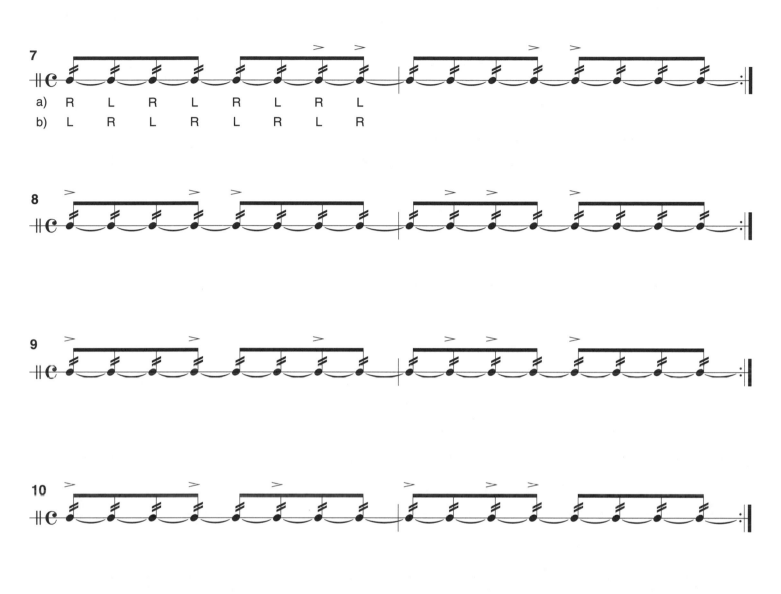

13

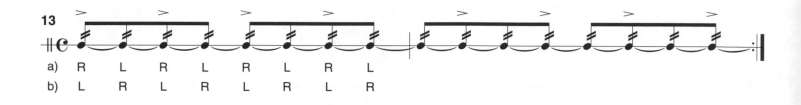

a) R L R L R L R L

b) L R L R L R L R

14

15

16

17

18

FOUR-BAR ROLL PATTERNS

Practice each of these four-bar patterns at least five times before proceeding. Be sure to practice leading with each hand (stickings a and b).

1

a)   R L R L R L R L
b)   L R L R L R L R

2

3

4

5

6

7

a) R L R L R L R L
b) L R L R L R L R

8

9

10

11

12

This thirty-two-bar 8th-note roll solo, and the three that follow, use many of the previously studied accent patterns. These exercises should be practiced leading with the left and right hands as indicated, and with the bass drum on all accented notes. Start slowly and increase speed gradually.

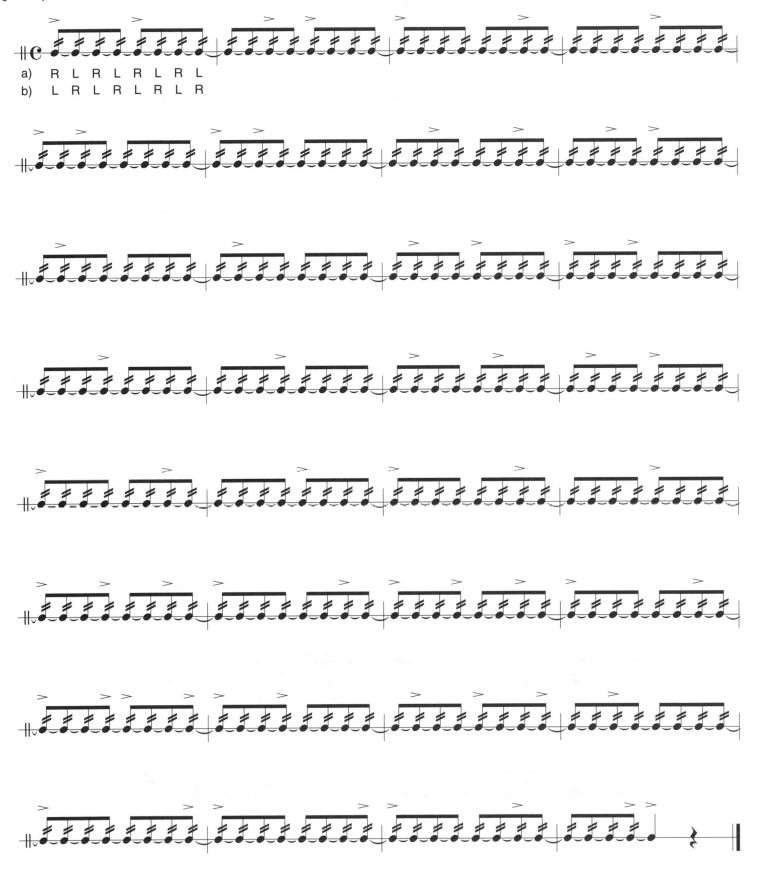

a)   R L R L R L R L
b)   L R L R L R L R

a) R L R L R L R L
b) L R L R L R L R

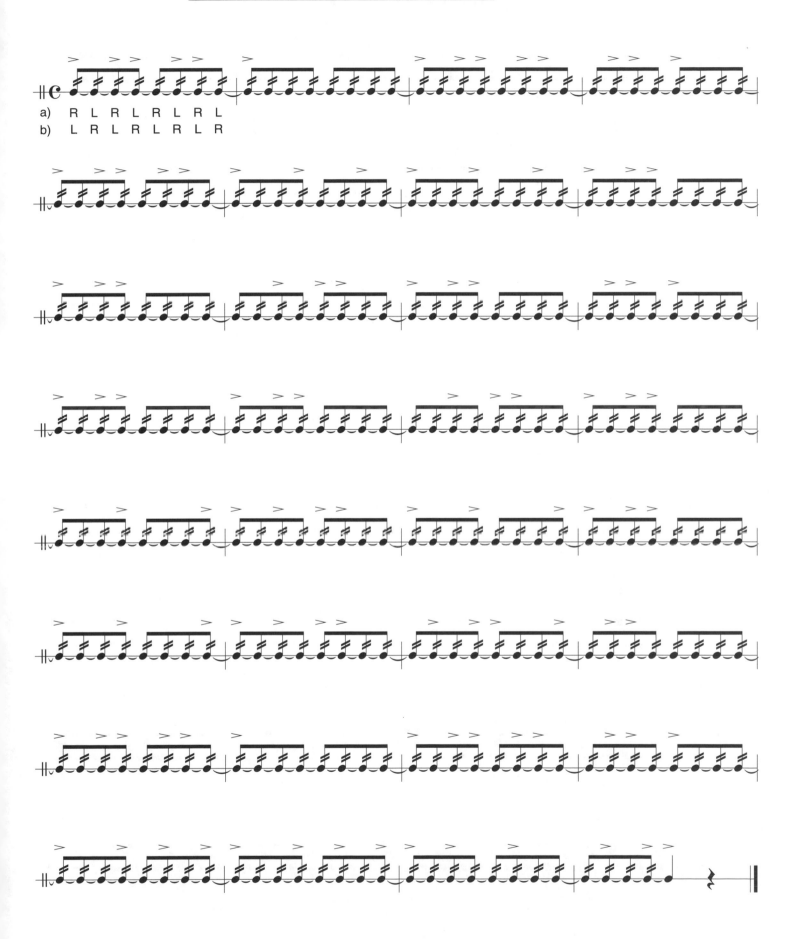

a) R L R L R L R L
b) L R L R L R L R

a) R L R L R L R L
b) L R L R L R L R

PART 2: TRIPLET ACCENTS

All of the triplet accent patterns on the following pages use sticking variations a, b, c, and d shown below. The other examples demonstrate optional ways the patterns can be played. 1) Add the bass drum on all accents. 2) Play all accents as rimshots. 3) Play all accents as flams. 4) Play all accents using snare drum, small tom-tom, and large tom-tom. Practice all of the material in Part 2 using each of the methods described below.

Sticking
Variations
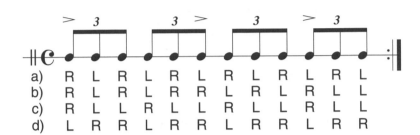

1) Add Bass Drum
   On Accents
   (Use All Stickings)
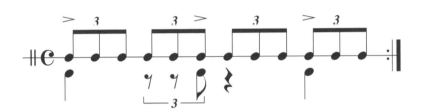

2) Play Accents
   As Rimshots
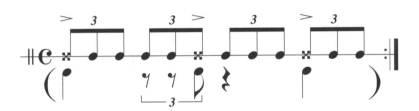

3) Play Accents
   As Flams
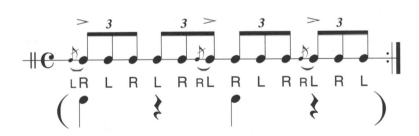

4) Drum To Drum
   (Alternate sticking
   only. Non-accents
   on snare drum,
   accented rights on
   large tom-tom,
   accented lefts on
   small tom-tom.)
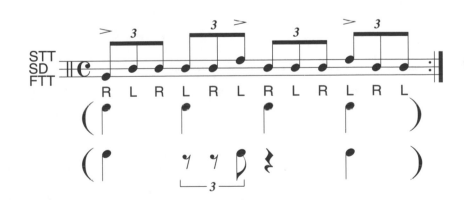

ONE-BAR PATTERNS

The 128 triplet accent patterns that follow should be practiced using stickings a, b, c, and d below. Be sure to practice all the patterns using the various systems described on page 39. Practice each exercise slowly at first and gradually increase the tempo as your fluency with each pattern improves. Also, be sure to make a strong distinction between all accented and unaccented notes.

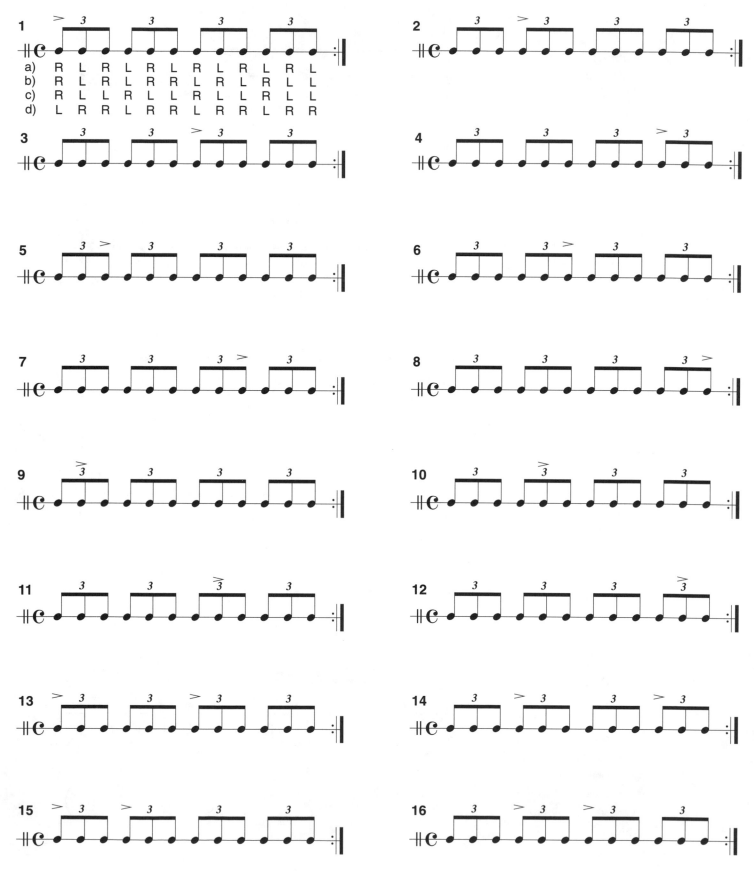

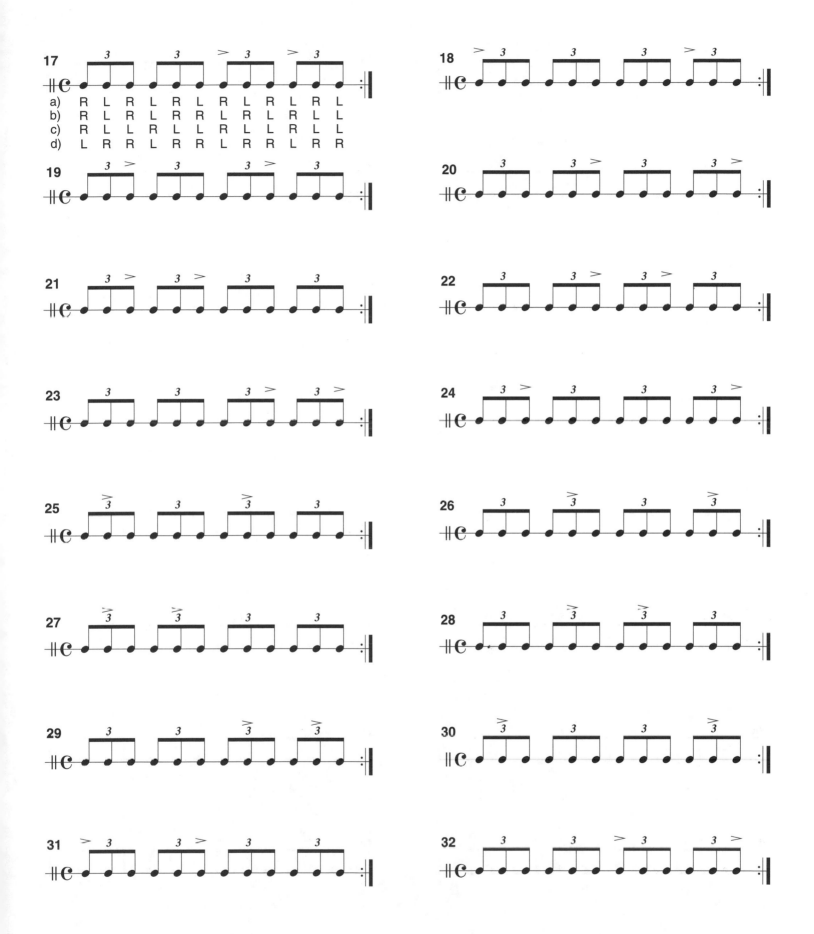

41

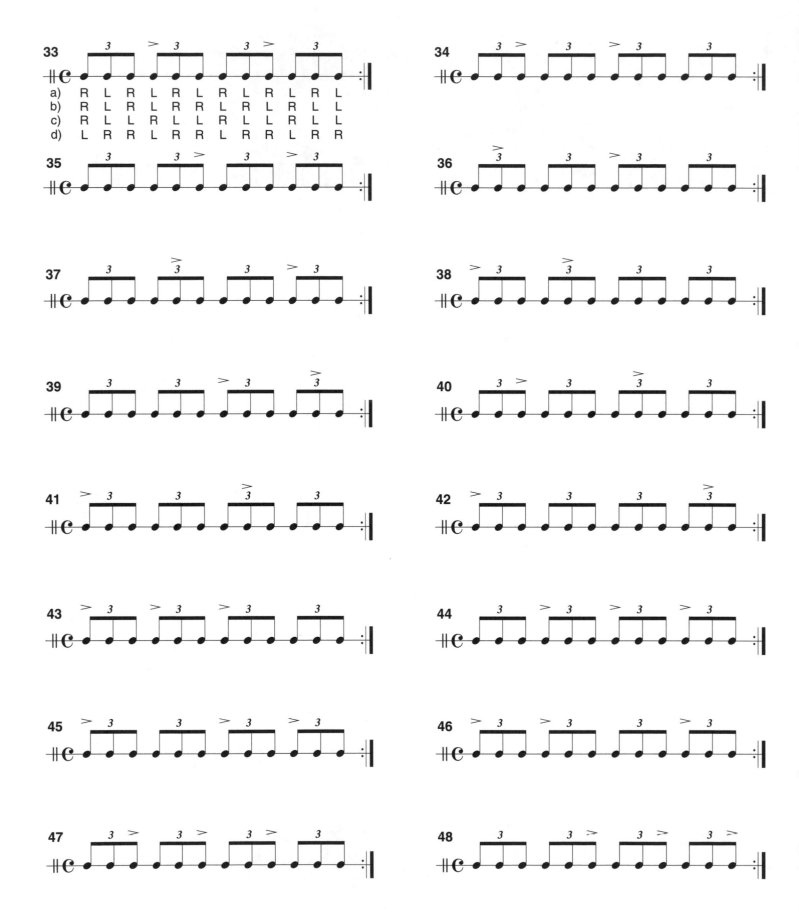

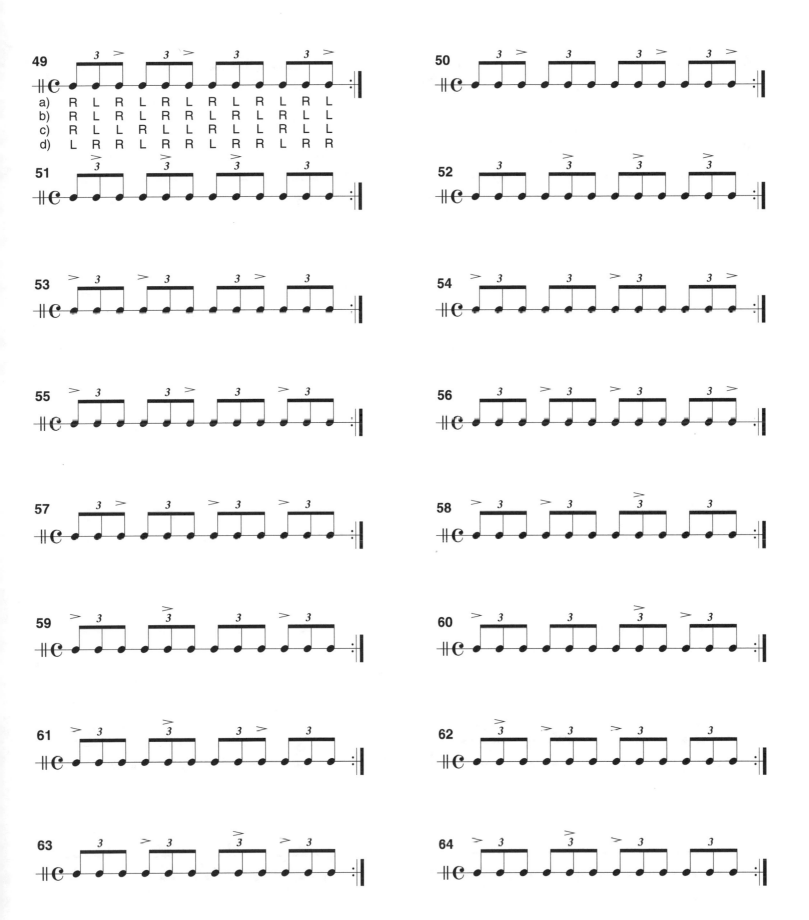

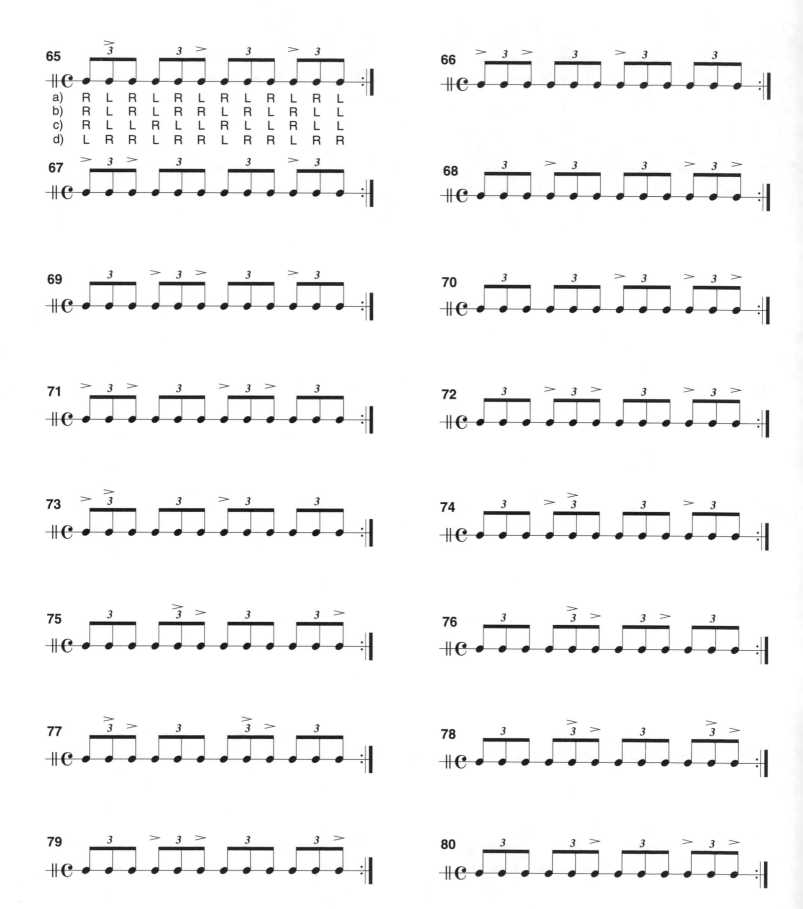

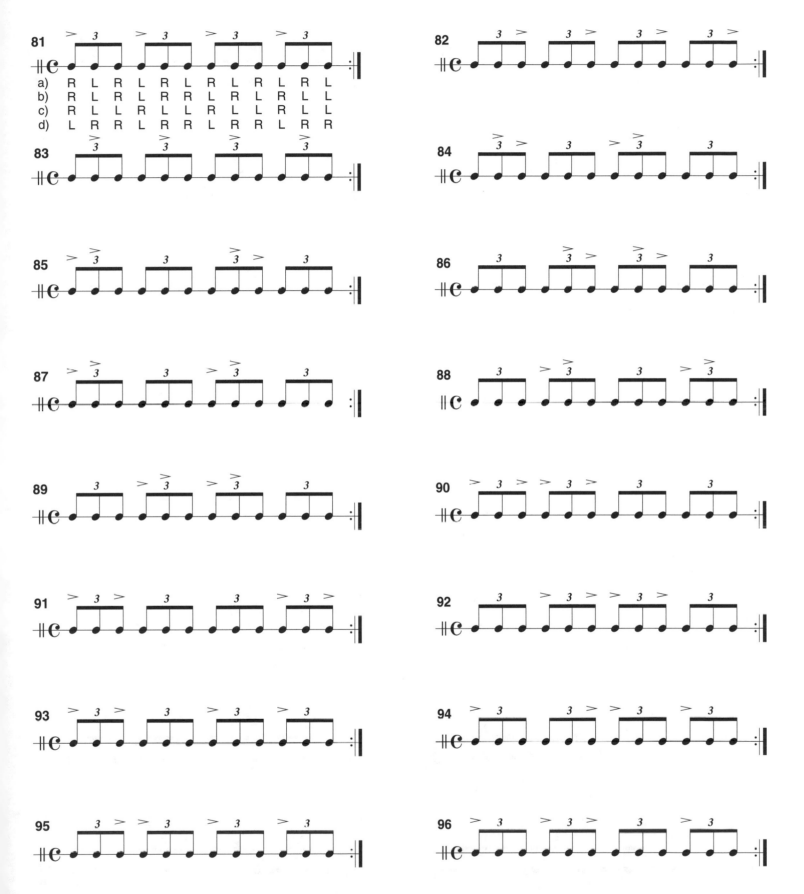

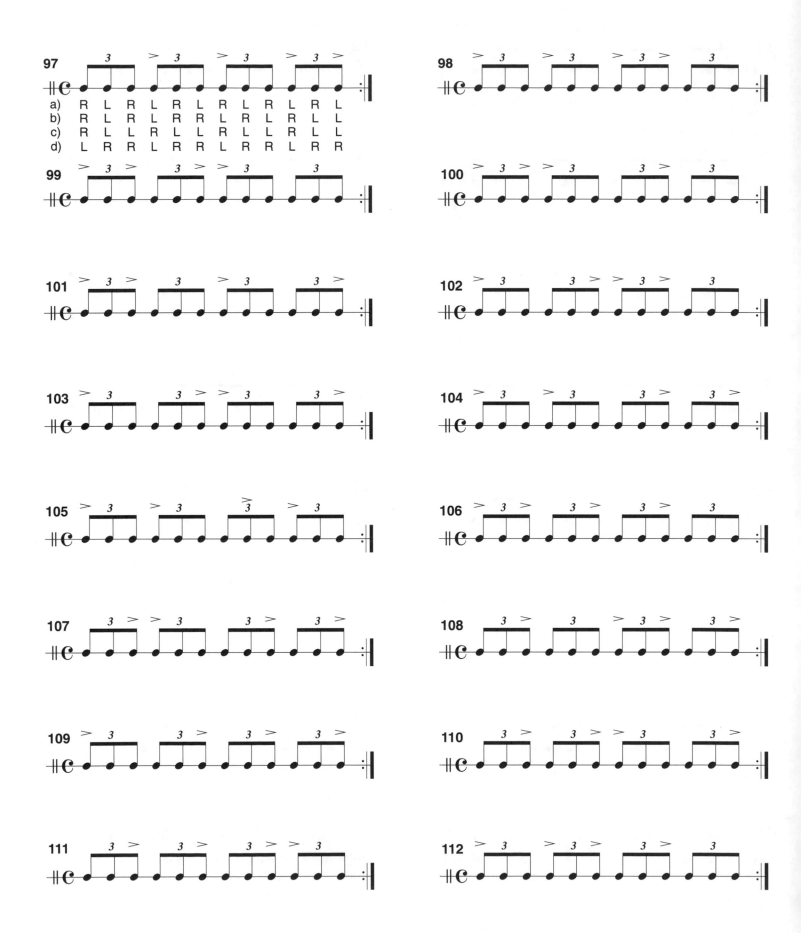

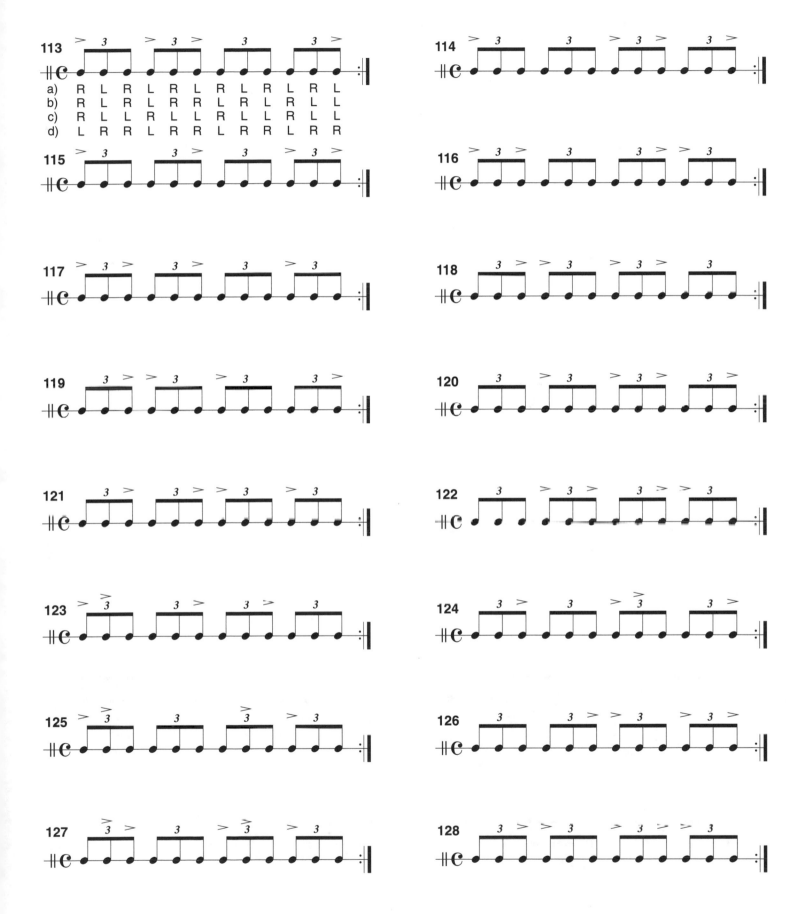

TWO-BAR PATTERNS

Practice these two-bar patterns in a similar manner to the one-bar exercises, using all of the varied methods described previously.

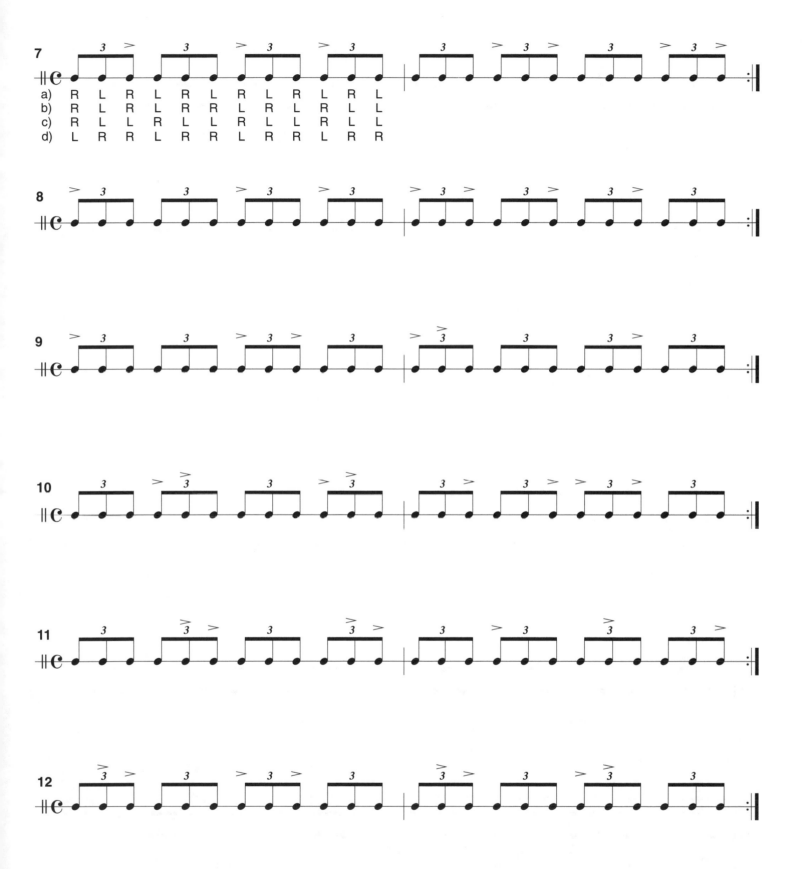

FOUR-BAR PATTERNS

Repeat each of these four-bar patterns at least five times before proceeding to the next one.

1
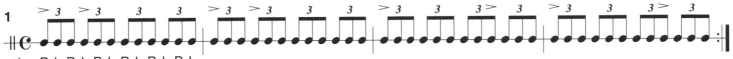

a) R L R L R L R L R L R L
b) R L R L R R L R L R L L
c) R L L R L L R L L R L L
d) L R R L R R L R R L R R

2

3

4

5

6

7

a) R L R L R L R L R L R L
b) R L R L R R L R L R L L
c) R L L R L L R L L R L L
d) L R R L R R L R R L R R

8

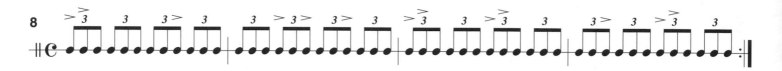

9

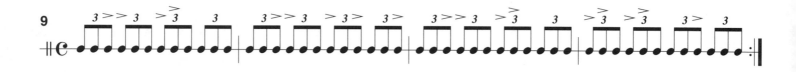

10

11

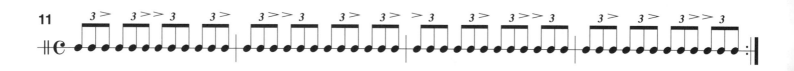

12

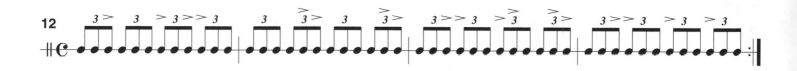

TRIPLET SOLO #1

This solo, and the three that follow, should be played using all four stickings. Then add the bass drum on all accented notes. Next, play all accents as rimshots with the bass drum, and then as alternating flams. Finally, using alternate sticking, practice the solos on the drums, playing non-accented notes on the snare drum, right-hand accents on large tom-tom, and left-hand accents on small tom-tom. Try these with the bass drum in four, and then with the bass drum on all accented notes. See page 39 at the beginning of this section for a further description.

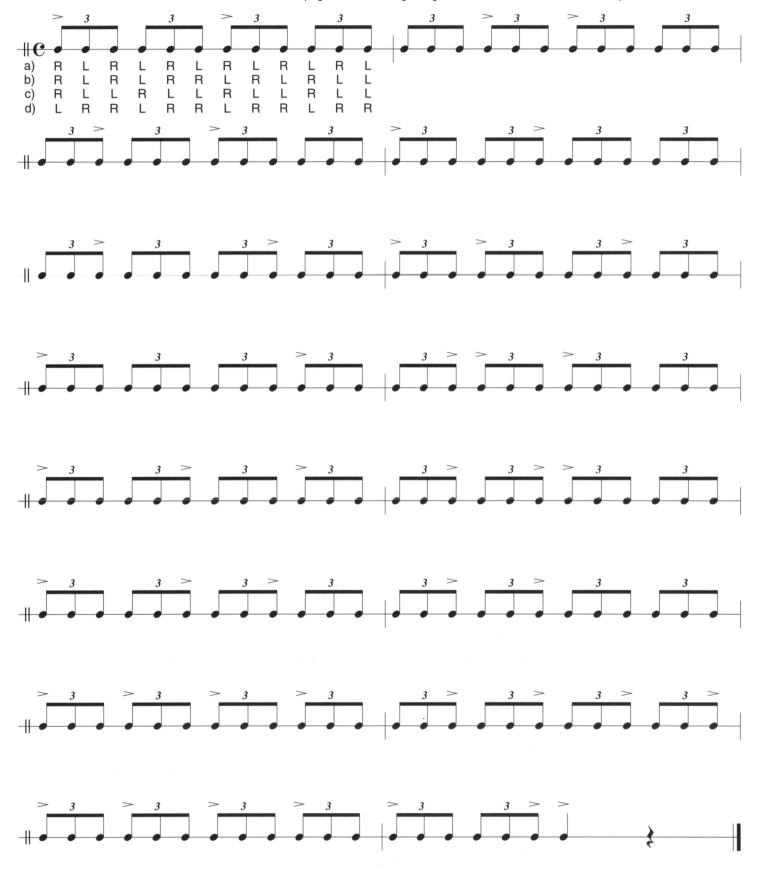

a) R L R L R L R L R L R L
b) R L R L R R L R L R L L
c) R L L R L L R L L R L L
d) L R R L R R L R R L R R

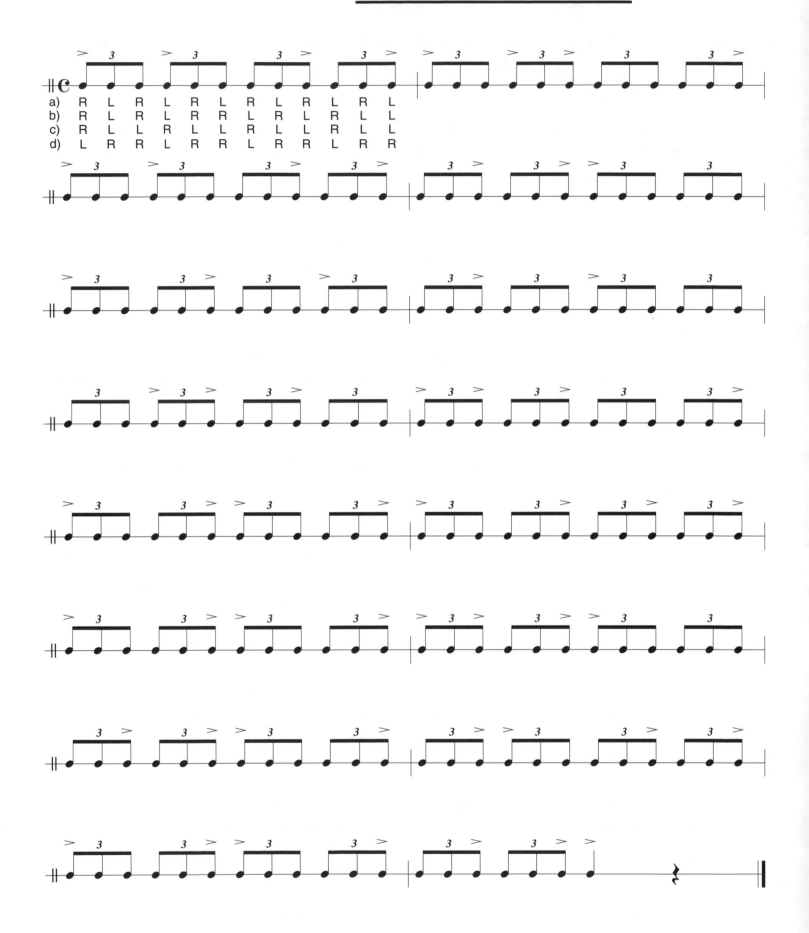

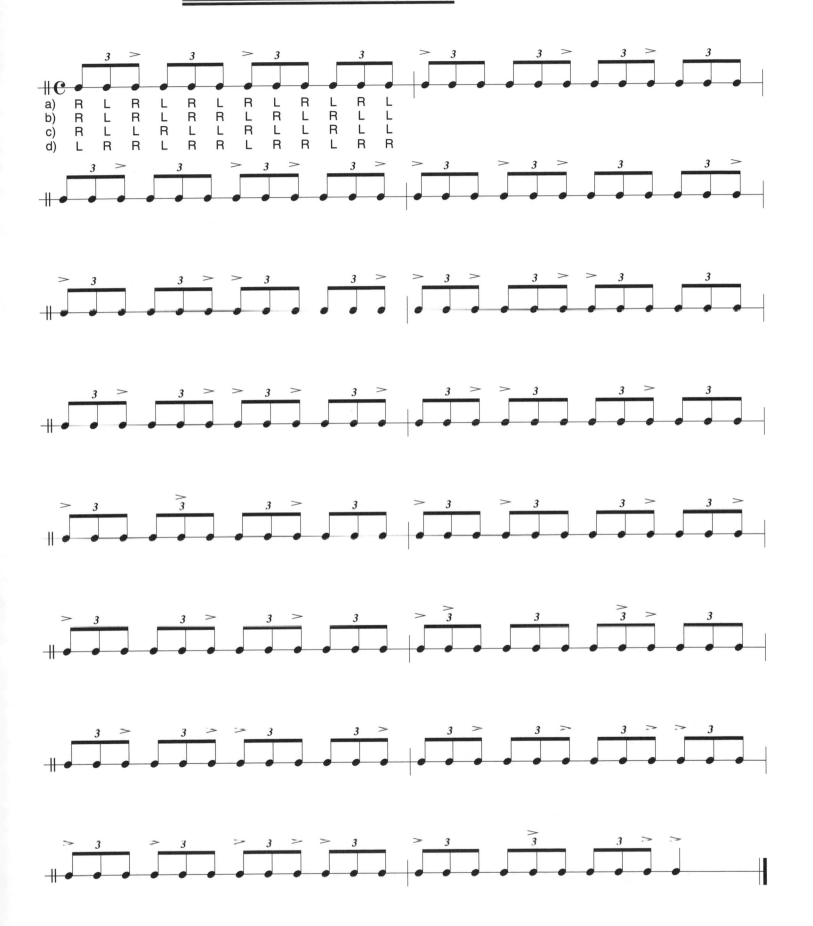

TRIPLET SOLO #4

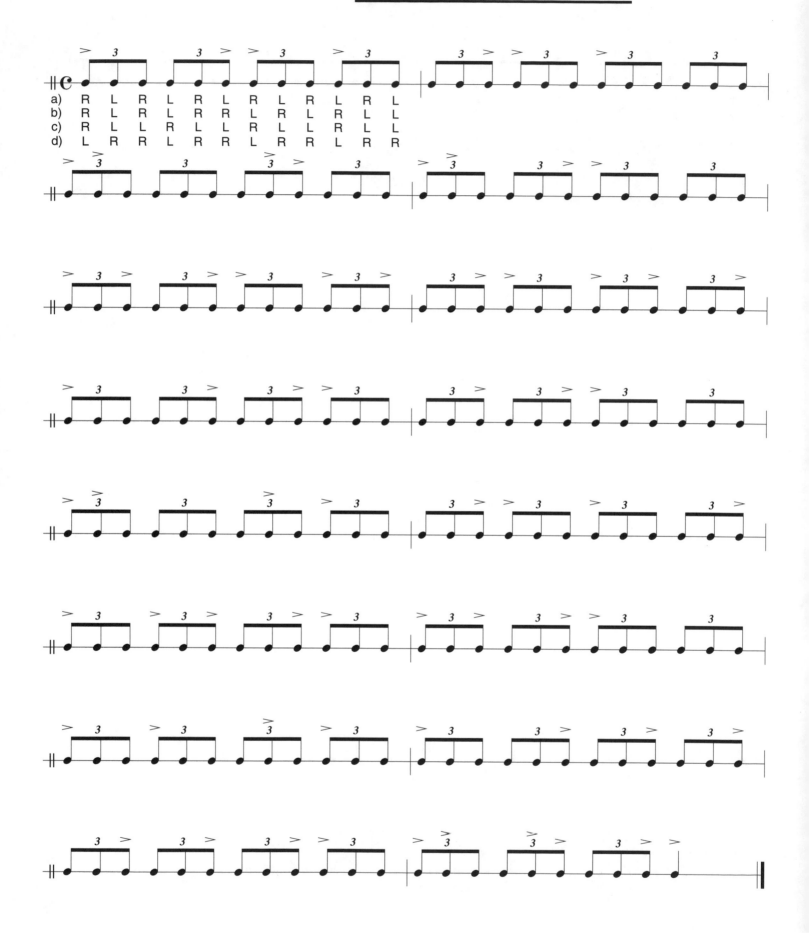

56

Each of the following triplet roll patterns should be played using a closed buzz roll. Be sure to make a strong distinction between the accented and unaccented buzz roll strokes. These patterns should also be practiced with the bass drum on all accented notes as shown below.

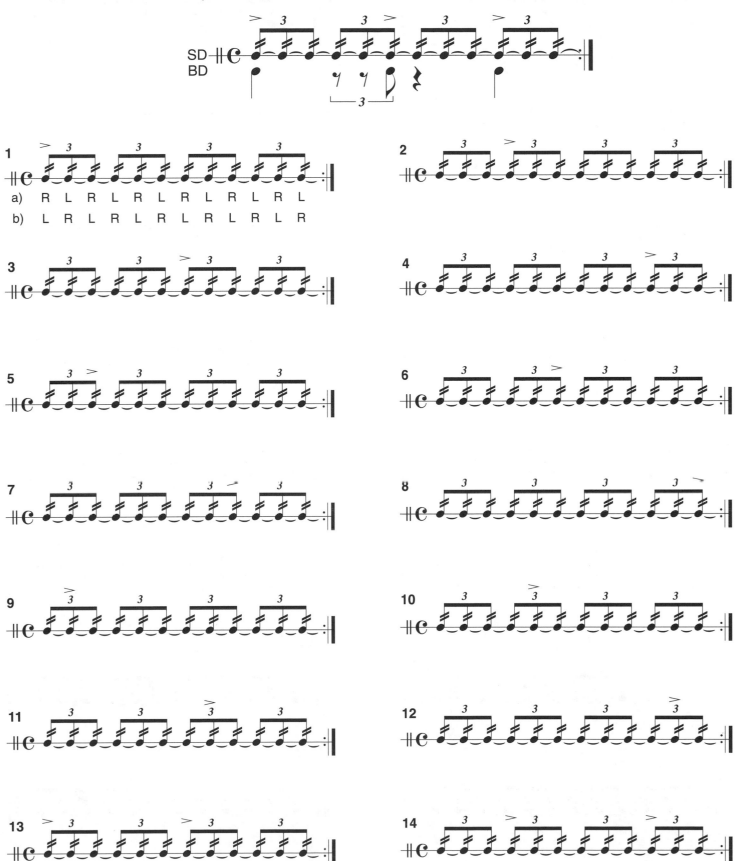

1
a) R L R L R L R L R L R L
b) L R L R L R L R L R L R

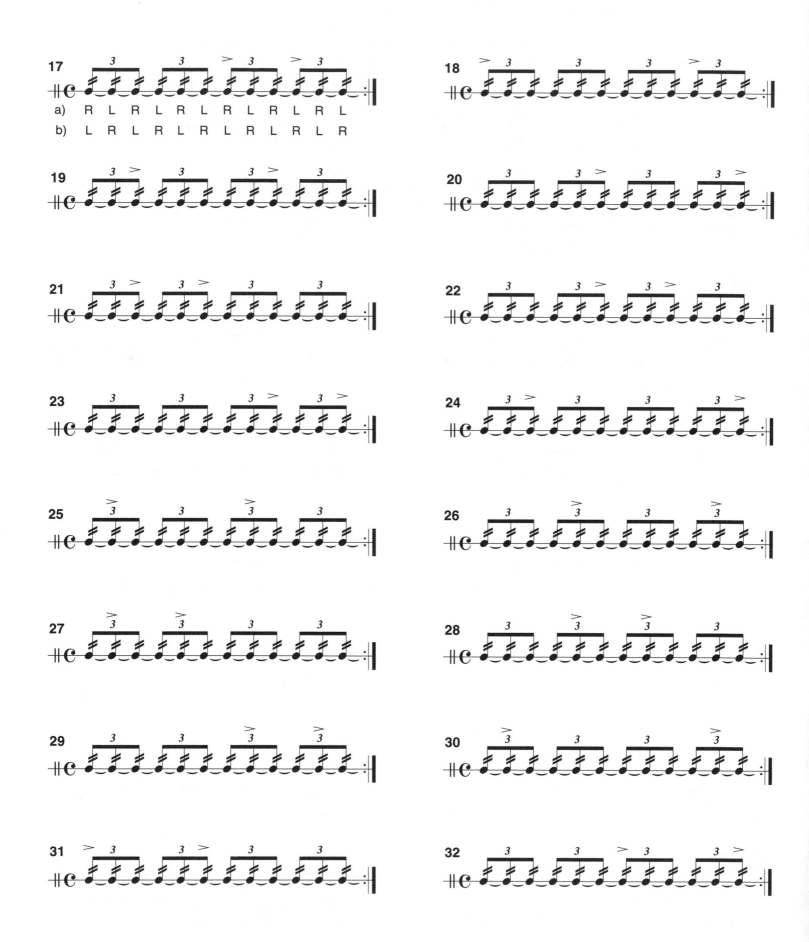

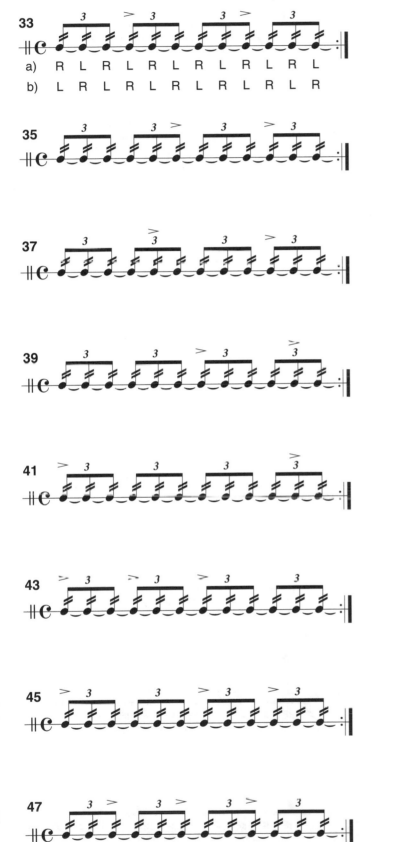
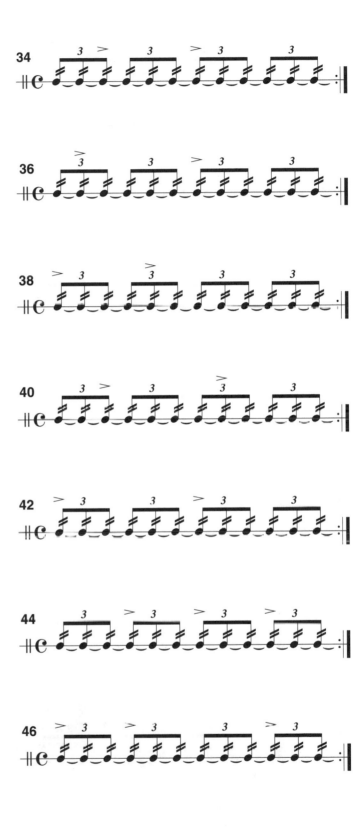

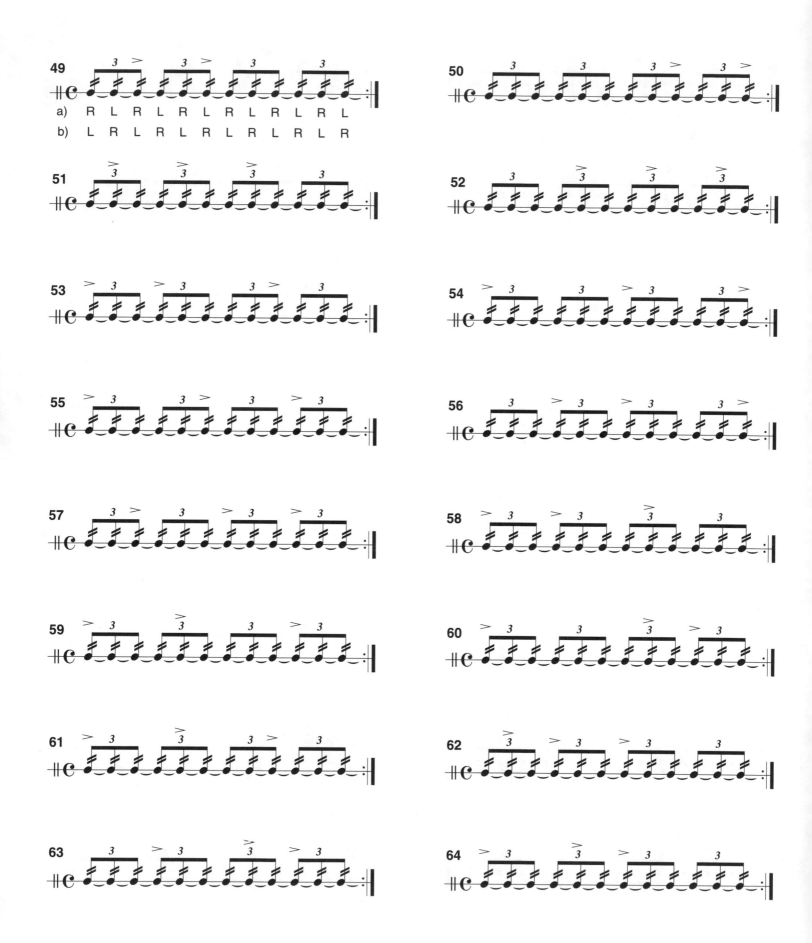

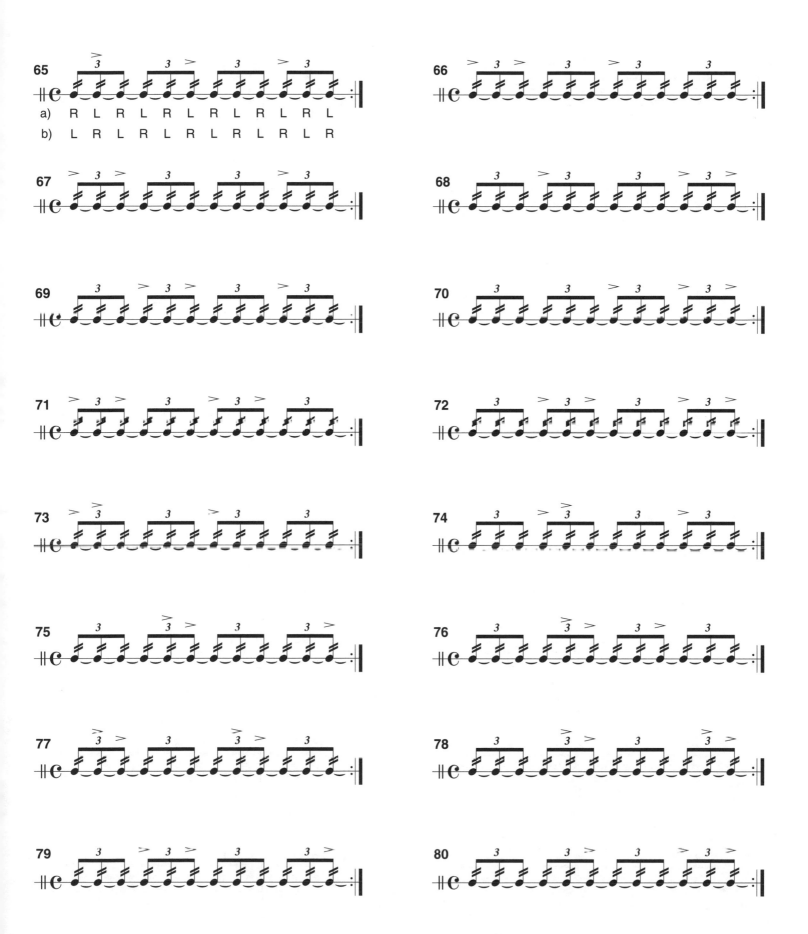

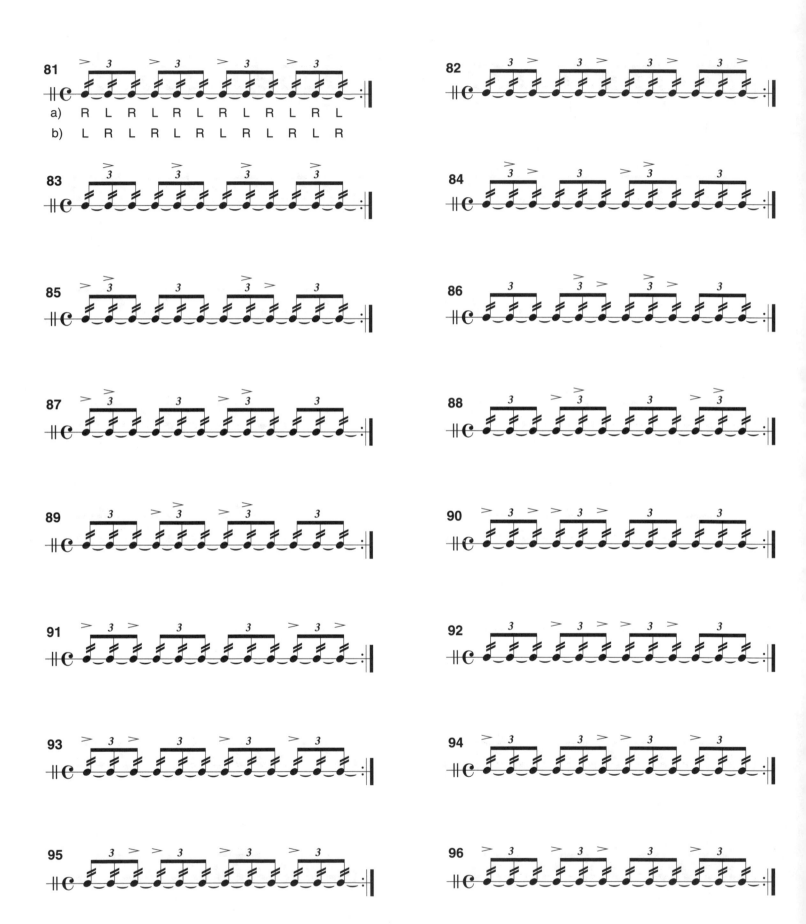

81
a) R L R L R L R L R L R L
b) L R L R L R L R L R L R

62

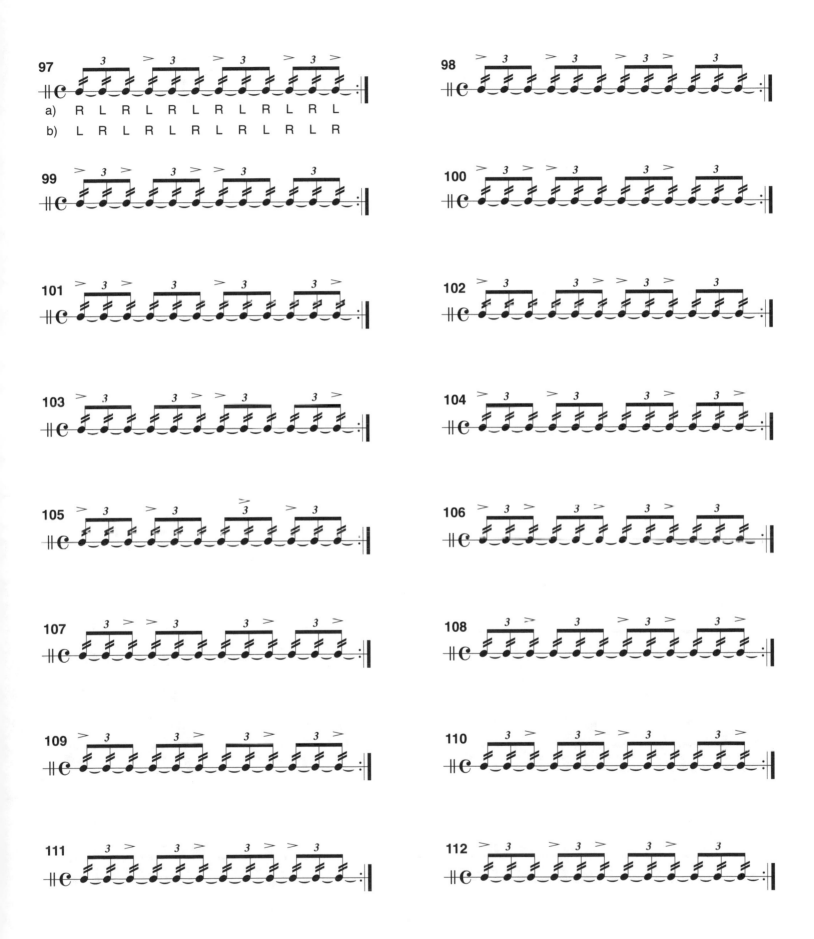

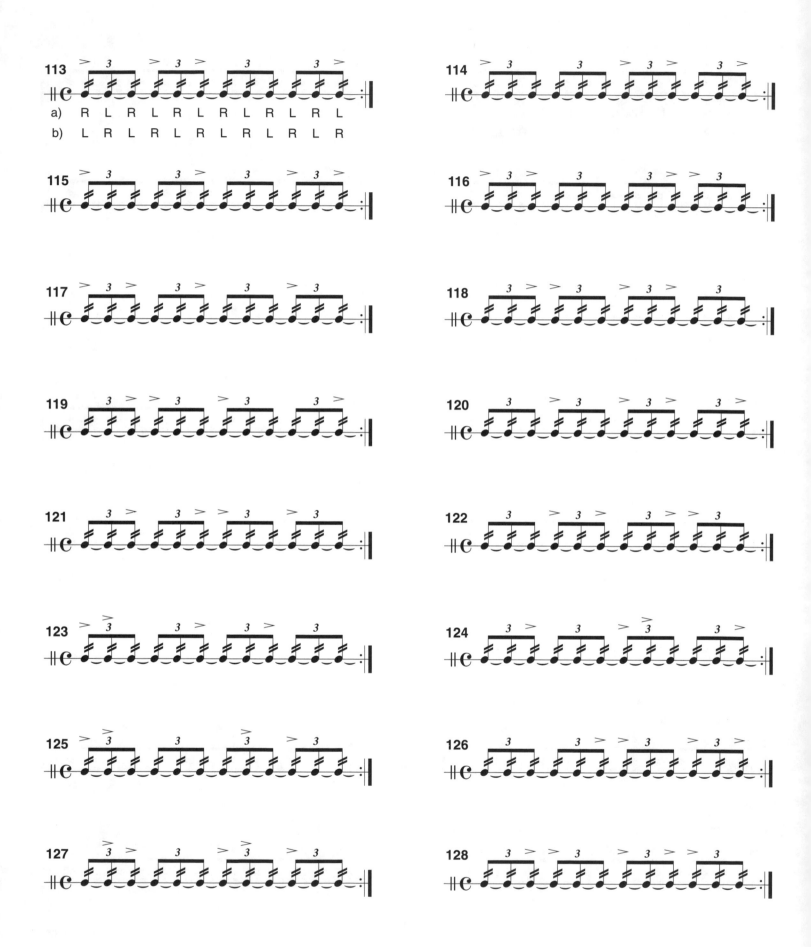

TWO-BAR ROLL PATTERNS

Take your time with these two-bar roll exercises. Increase speed gradually as your facility improves.

1

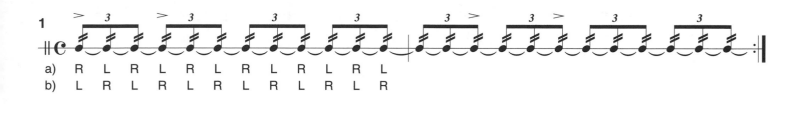

a) R L R L R L R L R L R L

b) L R L R L R L R L R L R

2

3

4

5

6

7

a) R L R L R L R L R L R L
b) L R L R L R L R L R L R

8

9

10

11

12

a) R L R L R L R L R L R L
b) L R L R L R L R L R L R

FOUR-BAR ROLL PATTERNS

Practice each of these four-bar patterns at least five times before proceeding. Be sure to practice leading with each hand (stickings a and b).

1

a) R L R L R L R L R L R L
b) L R L R L R L R L R L R

2

3

4

5

6

a) R L R L R L R L R L R L
b) L R L R L R L R L R L R

TRIPLET ROLL SOLO #1

This sixteen-bar triplet roll solo, and the three that follow, use many of the previously studied triplet accent patterns. Practice leading both with right and left hands, and then add the bass drum on all accented notes. Start slowly and increase speed gradually.

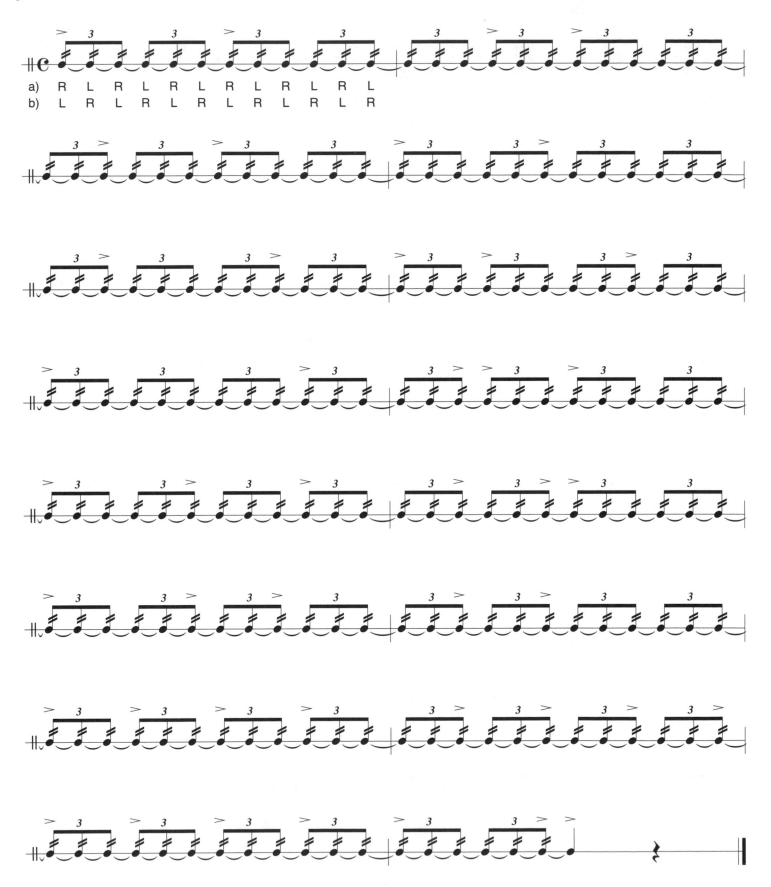

a) R L R L R L R L R L R L R L R L

b) L R L R L R L R L R L R L R L R

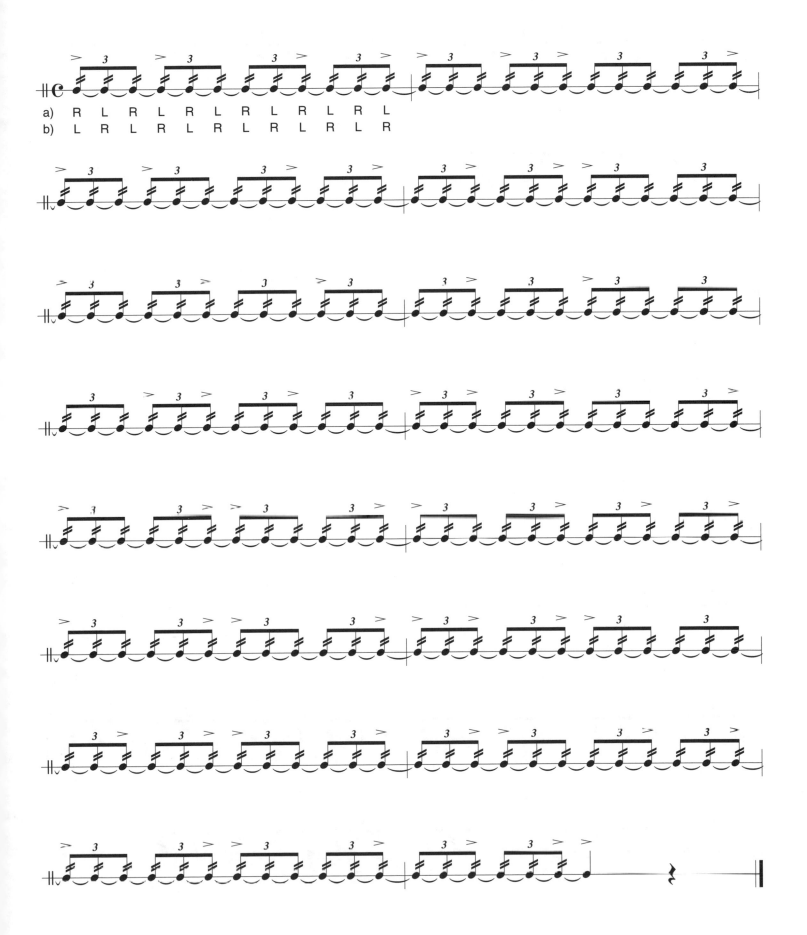

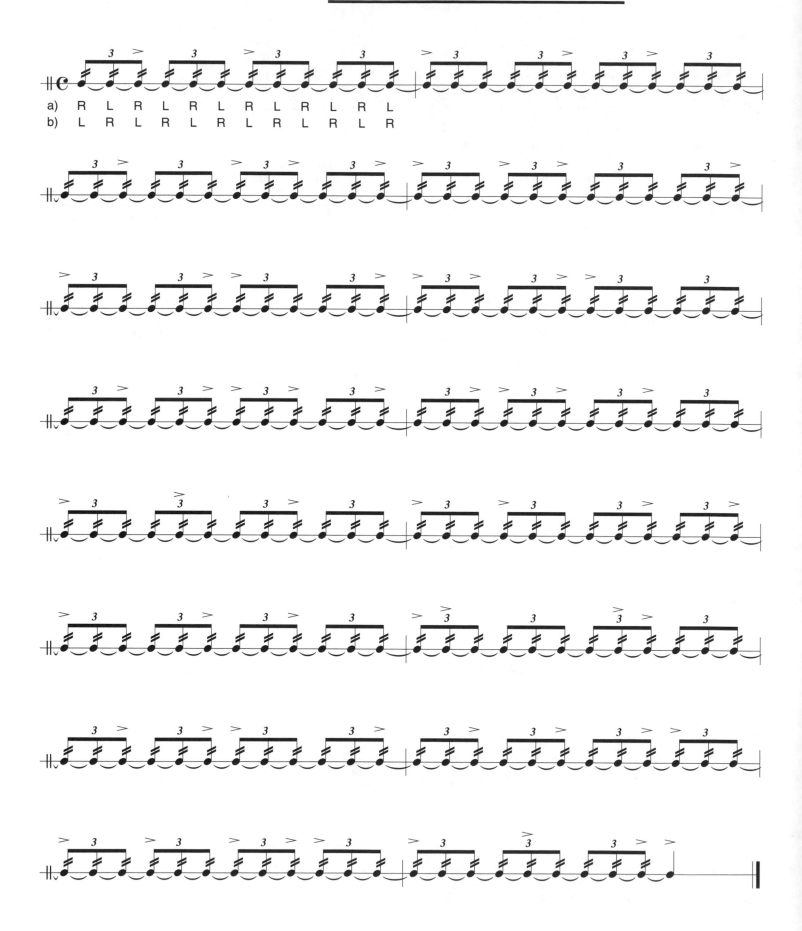

a) R L R L R L R L R L R L
b) L R L R L R L R L R L R

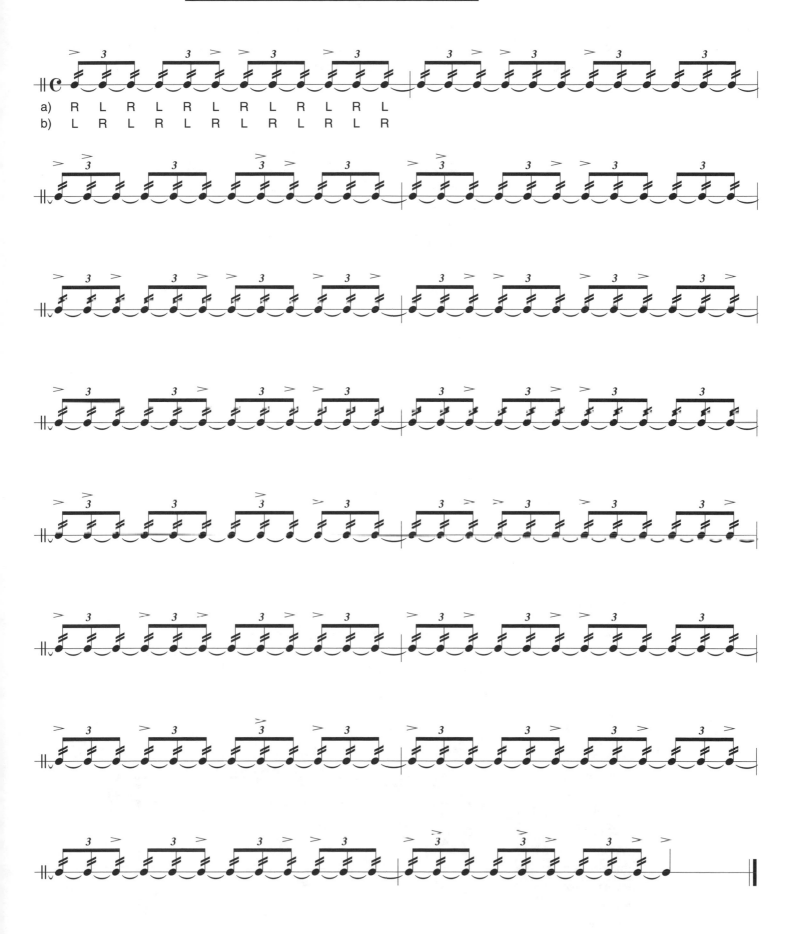

a) R L R L R L R L R L R L

b) L R L R L R L R L R L R

PART 3: 16TH-NOTE ACCENTS

All of the 16th-note accent patterns on the following pages use sticking variations a, b, c, and d shown below. The other examples demonstrate optional ways the patterns can be played. 1) Add the bass drum on all accents. 2) Play all accents as rimshots. 3) Play all accents as flams. 4) Play all accents using snare drum, small tom-tom, and large tom-tom. Practice all of the material in Part 3 using each of the methods described below.

Sticking Variations

1) Add Bass Drum On Accents

2) Play Accents As Rimshots

3) Play Accents As Flams

4) Drum To Drum (Alternate sticking only. Accented rights on large tom-tom, lefts on small tom-tom, non-accents on snare drum.)

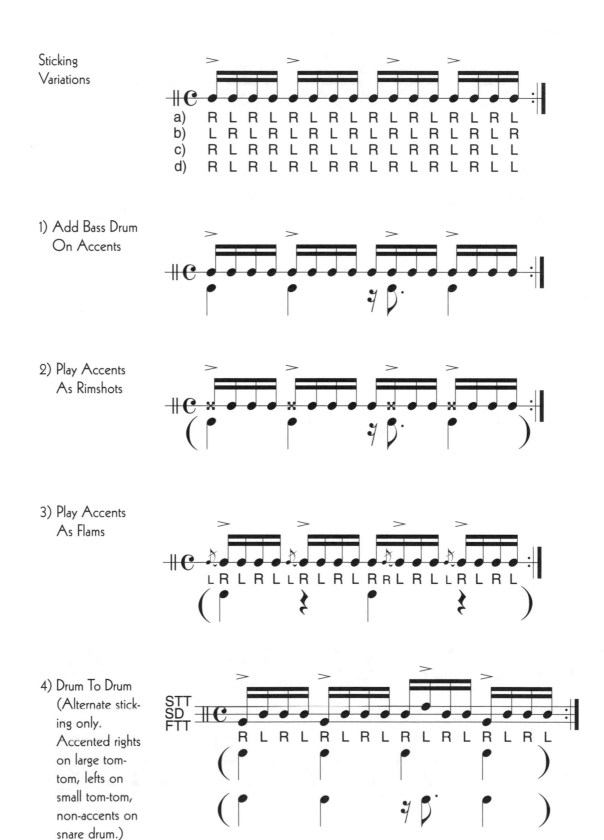

ONE-BAR PATTERNS

The 128 16th-note accent patterns that follow should be practiced using the four stickings shown: a) alternate sticking leading with the right hand, b) alternate sticking leading with the left hand, c) single paradiddle sticking, and d) triple paradiddle sticking.

Be sure to practice all of the patterns using the various systems described on page 74. Work each exercise slowly at first and gradually increase the tempo as your fluency improves. Also, be sure to make a strong distinction between all accented and unaccented notes.

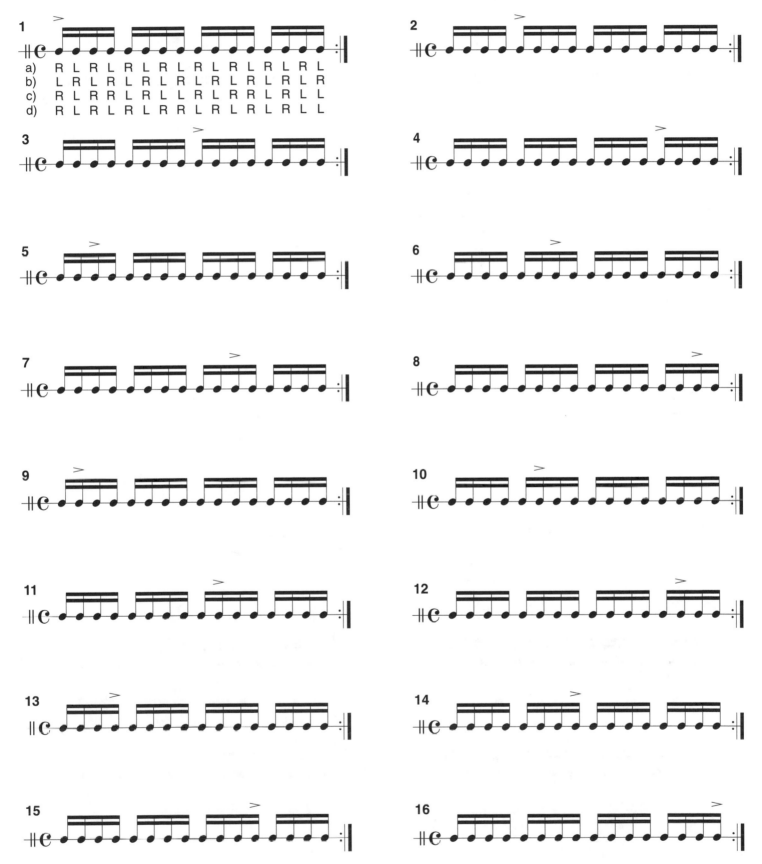

1
a) R L R L R L R L R L R L R L R L
b) L R L R L R L R L R L R L R L R
c) R L R R L R L L R L R R L R L L
d) R L R L R L R R L R L R L R L L

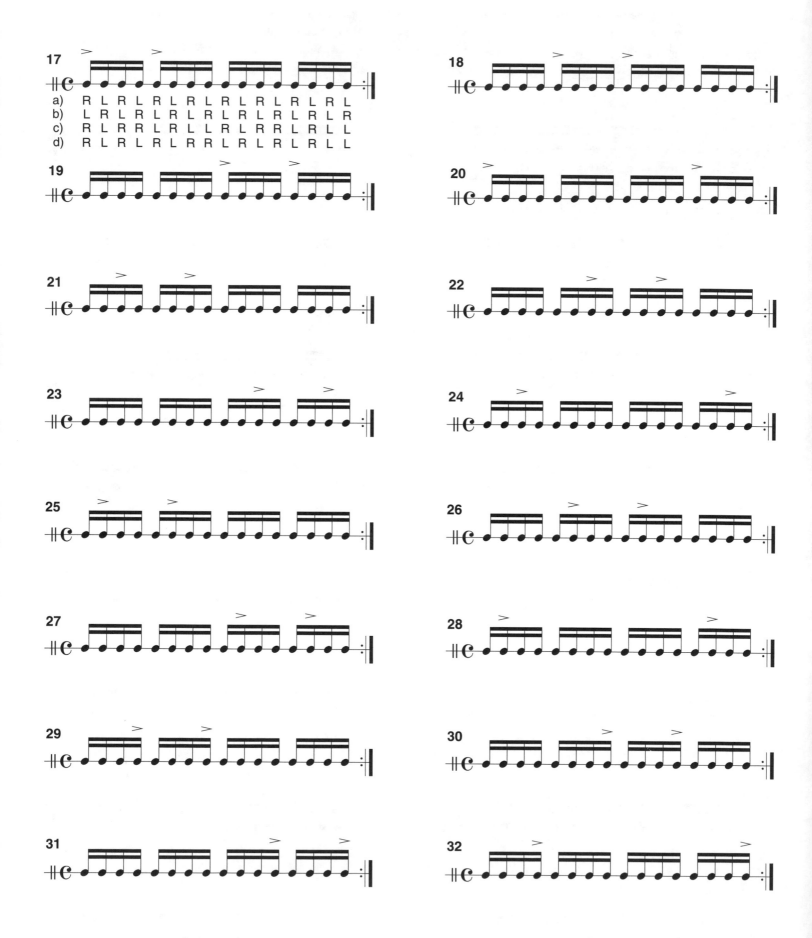

17
a) R L R L R L R L R L R L R L R L
b) L R L R L R L R L R L R L R L R
c) R L R R L R L L R L R R L R L L
d) R L R L R L R R L R L R L R L L

76

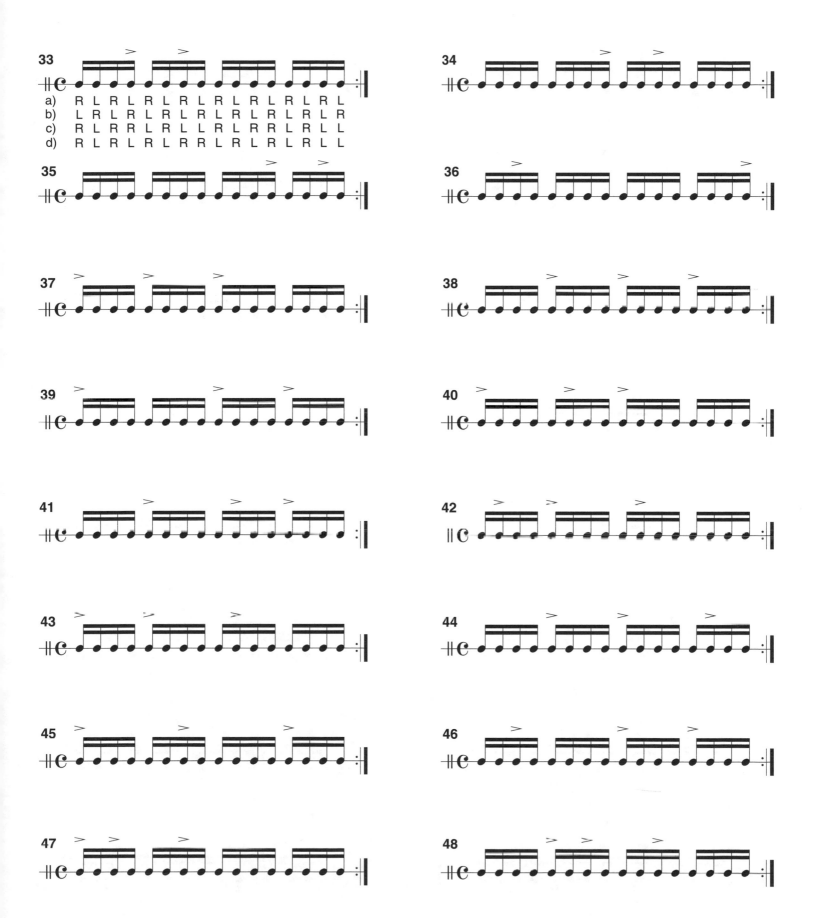

33
a) R L R L R L R L R L R L R L R L
b) L R L R L R L R L R L R L R L R
c) R L R R L R L L R L R R L R L L
d) R L R L R L R R L R L R L R L L

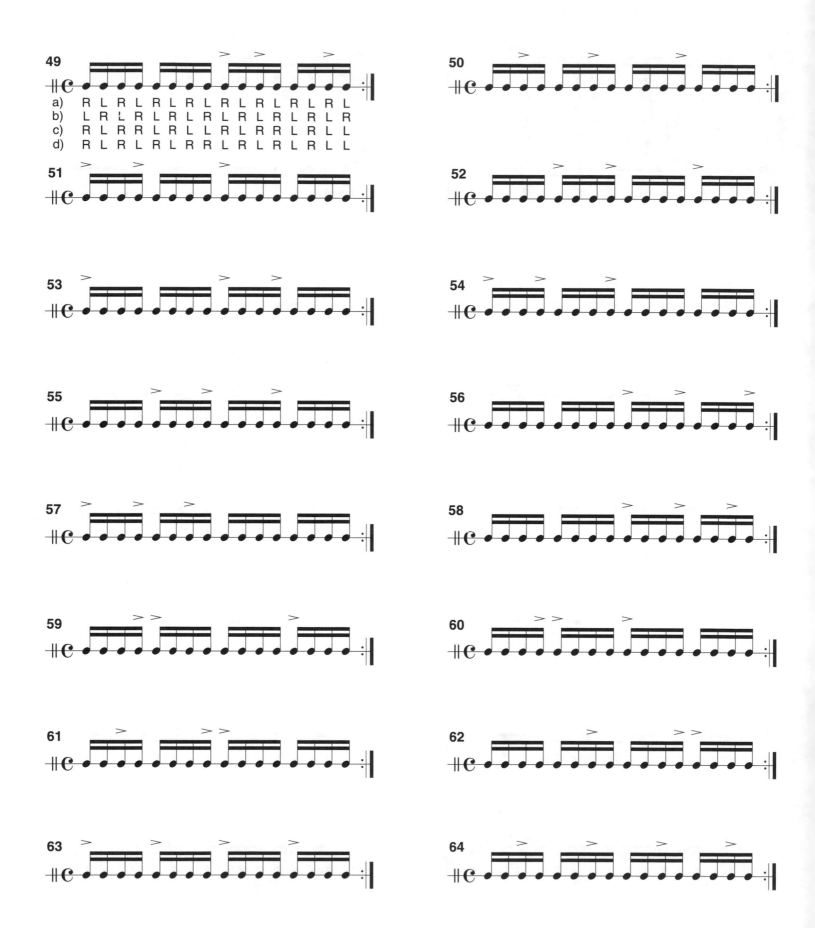

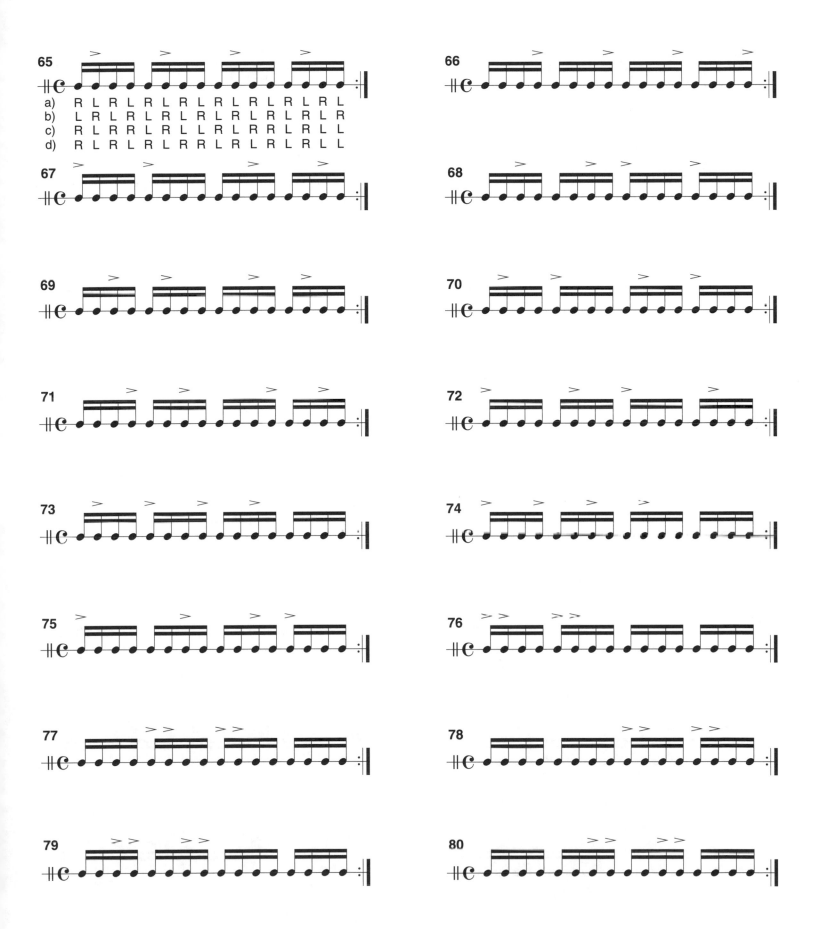

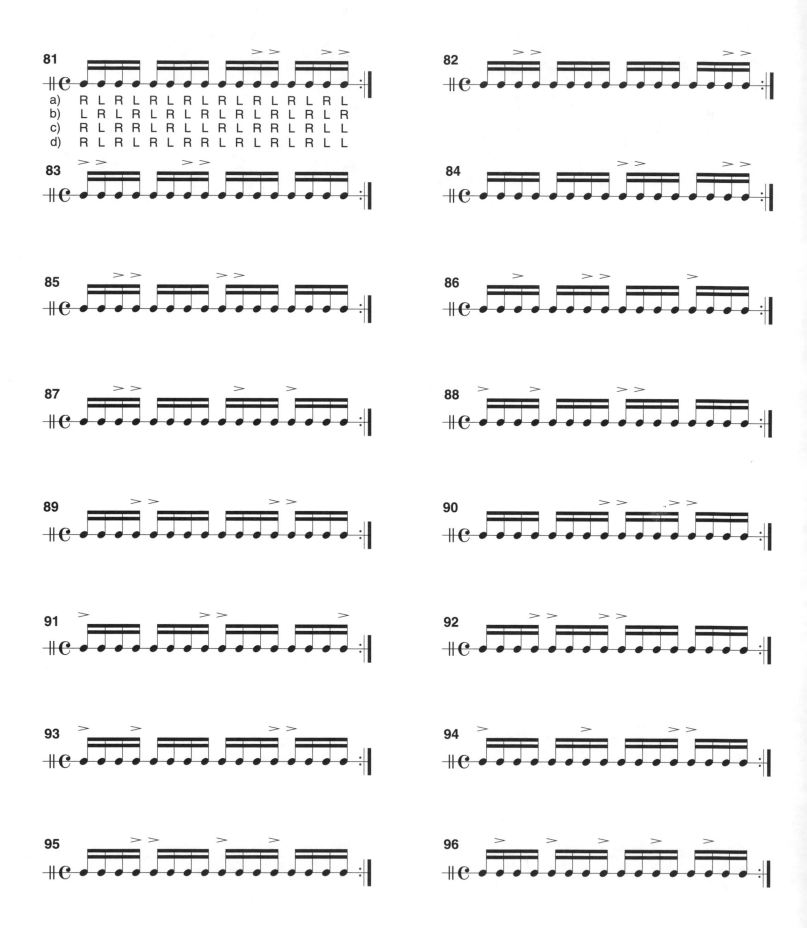

81
a) R L R L R L R L R L R L R L R L
b) L R L R L R L R L R L R L R L R
c) R L R R L R L L R L R R L R L L
d) R L R L R L R R L R L R L R L L

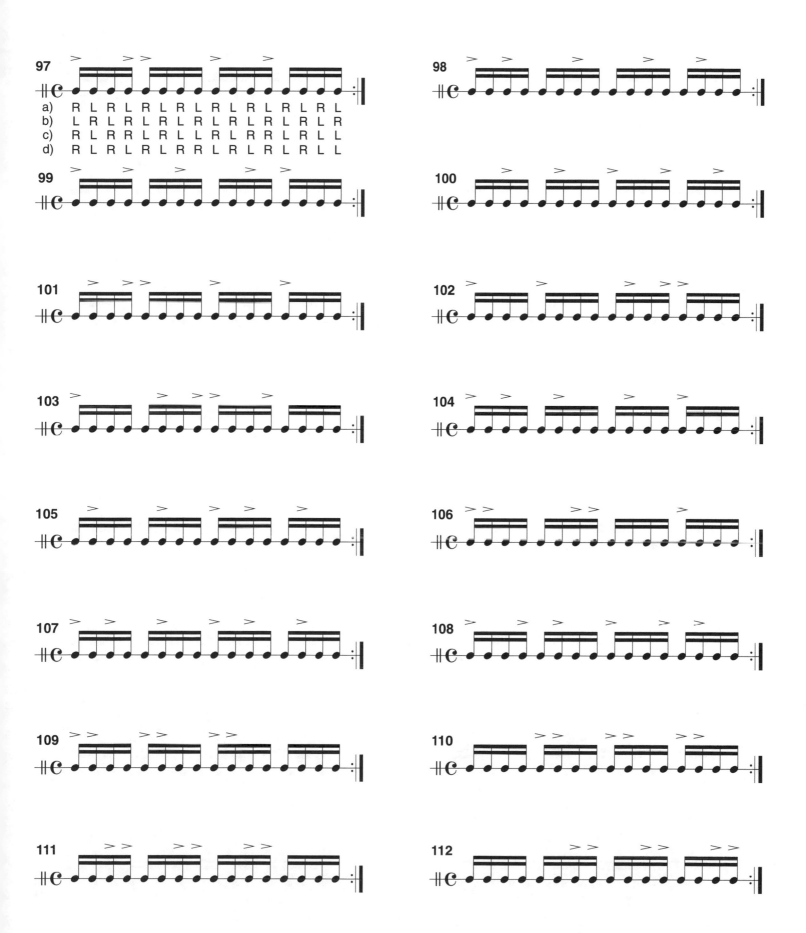

97

a) R L R L R L R L R L R L R L R L
b) L R L R L R L R L R L R L R L R
c) R L R R L R L L R L R R L R L L
d) R L R L R L R R L R L R L R L L

98

99

100

101

102

103

104

105

106

107

108

109

110

111

112

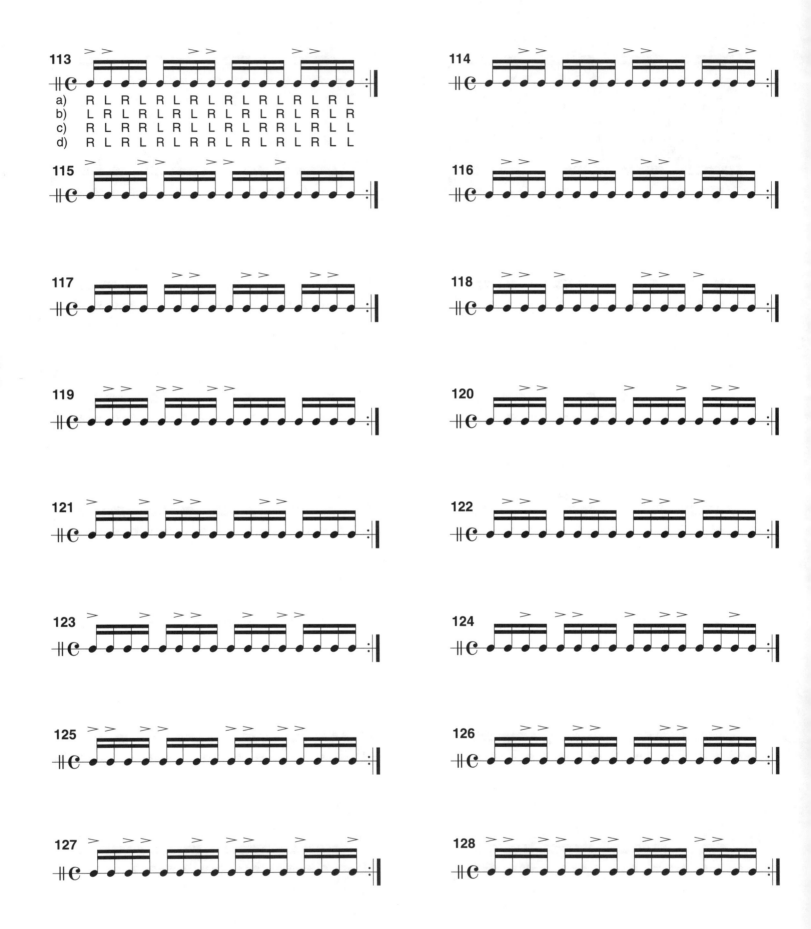

TWO-BAR PATTERNS

Practice these two-bar patterns in a similar manner to the one-bar exercises, using all of the varied methods described previously.

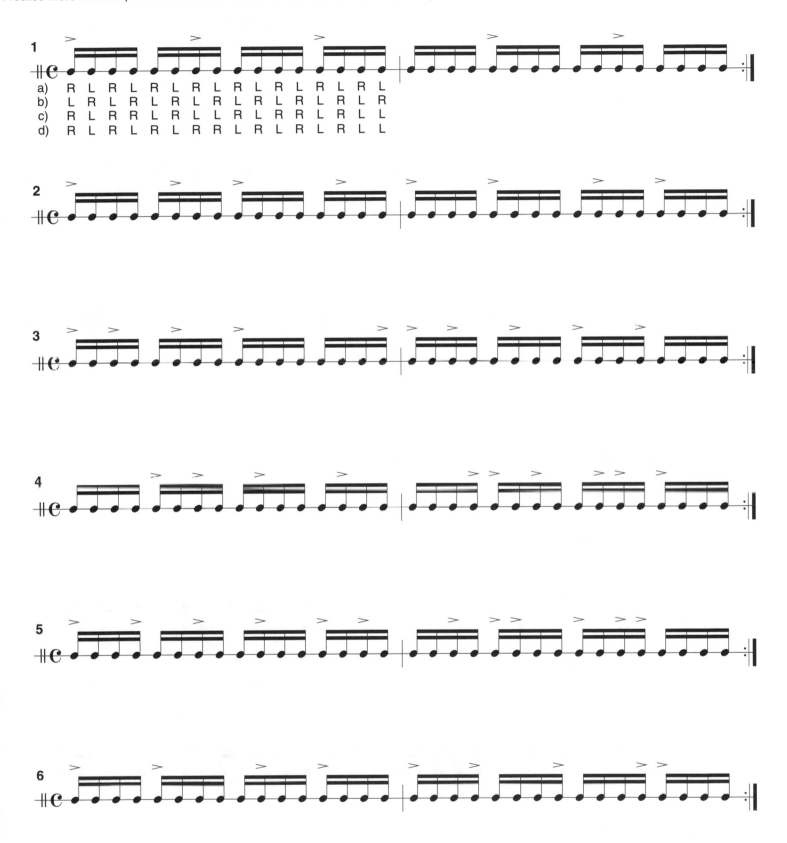

1

a) R L R L R L R L R L R L R L R L
b) L R L R L R L R L R L R L R L R
c) R L R R L R L L R L R R L R L L
d) R L R L R L R R L R L R L R L L

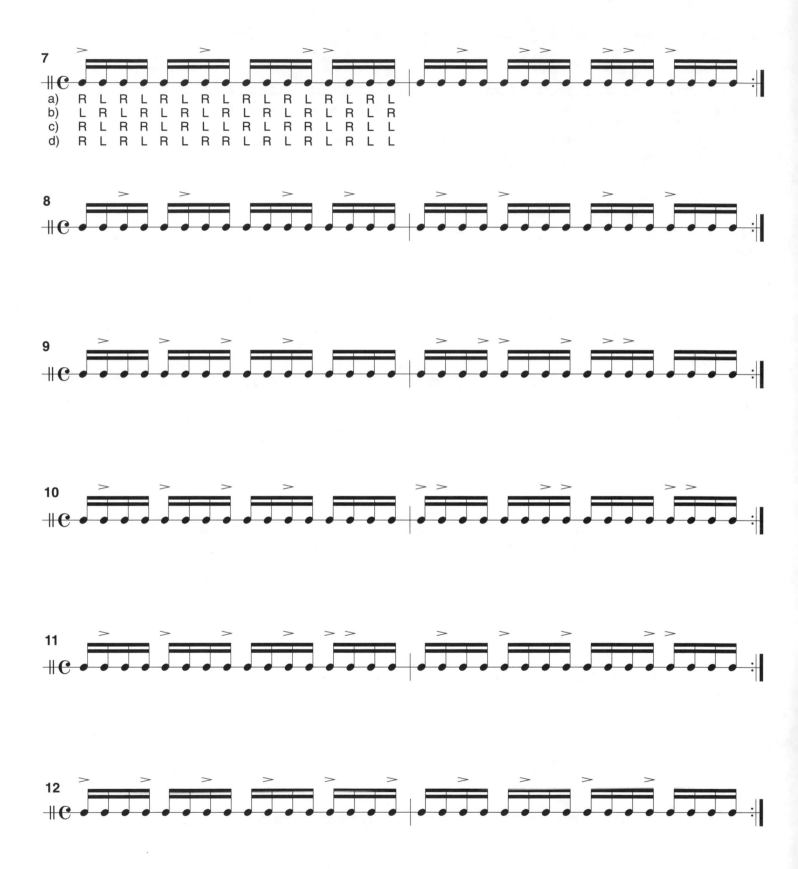

a) R L R L R L R L R L R L R L R L R L

b) L R L R L R L R L R L R L R L R L R

c) R L R R L R L L R L R R L R L L R L

d) R L R L R L R R L R L R L R L L L

84

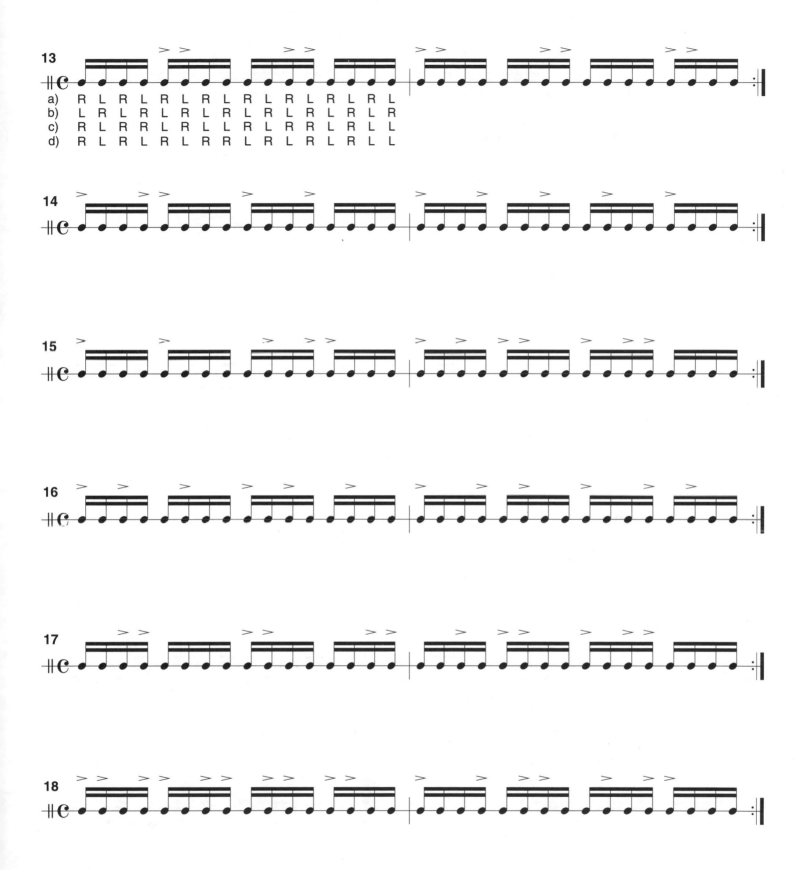

FOUR-BAR PATTERNS

Repeat each of the four-bar patterns at least five times before proceeding to the next one.

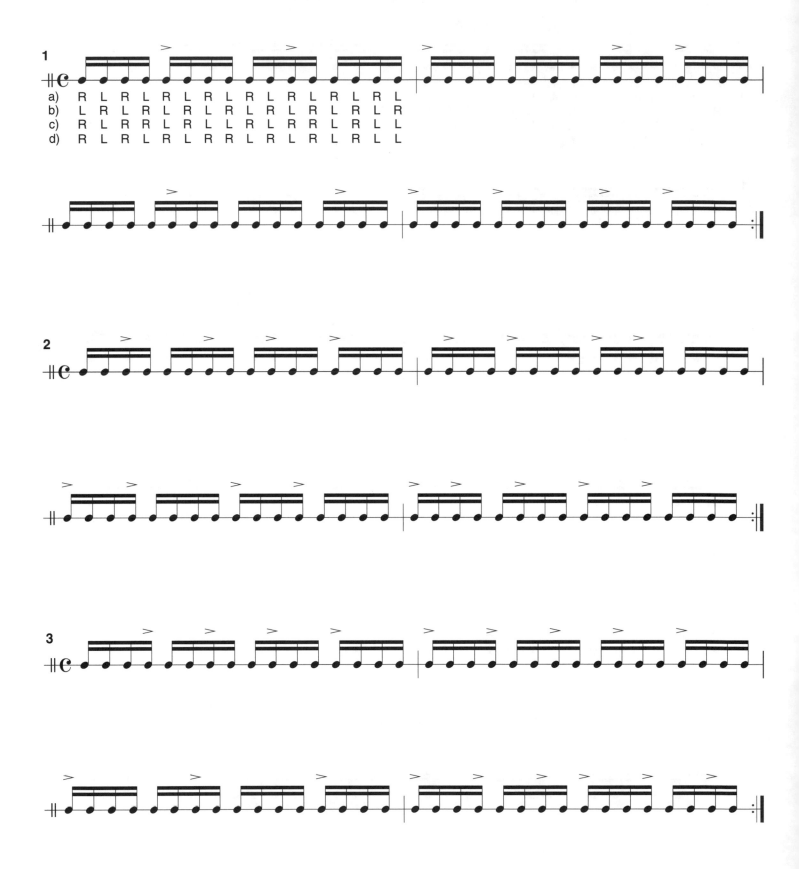

a) R L R L R L R L R L R L R L R L
b) L R L R L R L R L R L R L R L R
c) R L R R L R L L R L R R L R L L
d) R L R L R L R R L R L R L R L L

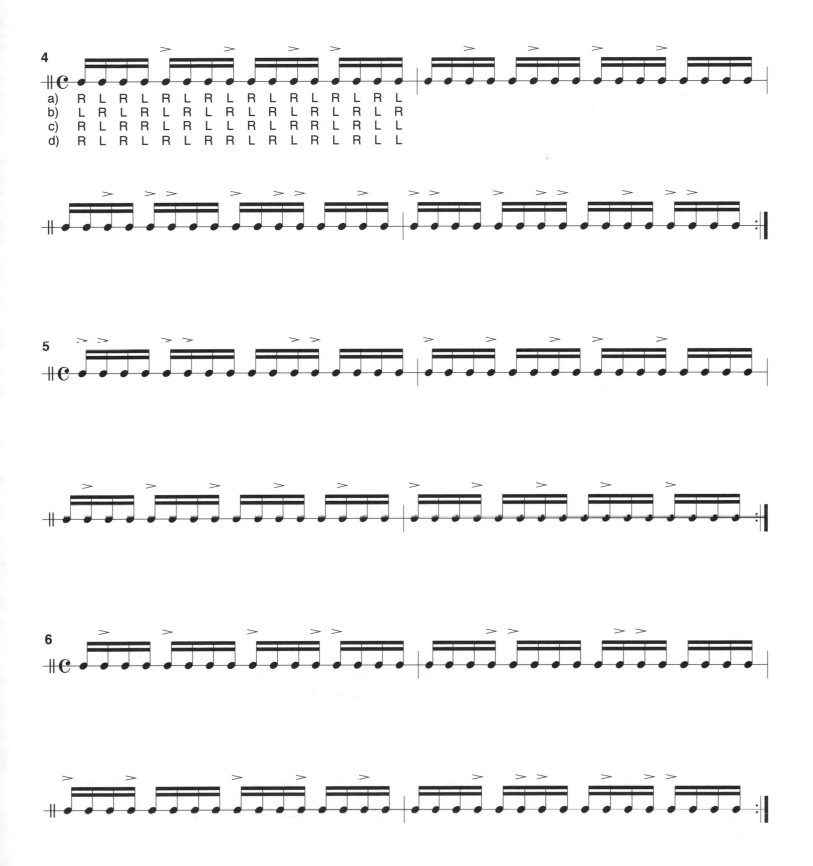

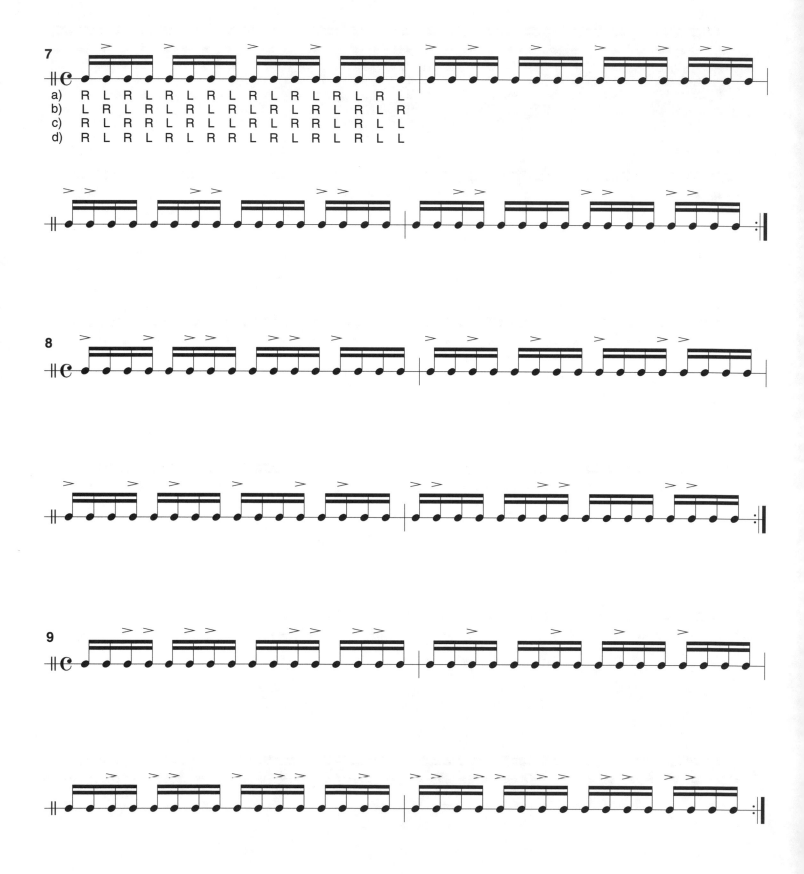

a) R L R L R L R L R L R L R L R L
b) L R L R L R L R L R L R L L R L R
c) R L R R L R L L R L R R L L R R L L
d) R L R L R L R R L R L R L R L L

16TH-NOTE SOLO #1

This solo, and the three that follow, should be played using all four stickings shown below. Next, play all accents as rimshots with the bass drum, and then as alternating flams. Finally, using alternate sticking, practice the four solos on the drumset, playing unaccented notes on snare drum, right-hand accents on large tom-tom, and left-hand accents on small tom-tom. Try these with the bass drum in four, and then with the bass drum on all accented notes. See page 74 at the beginning of this section for further description.

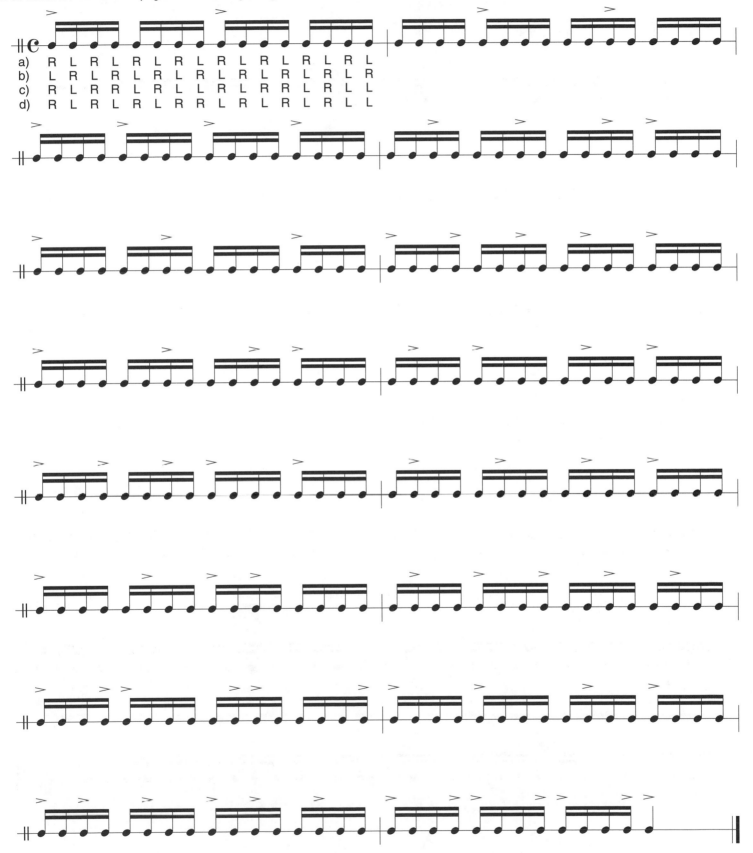

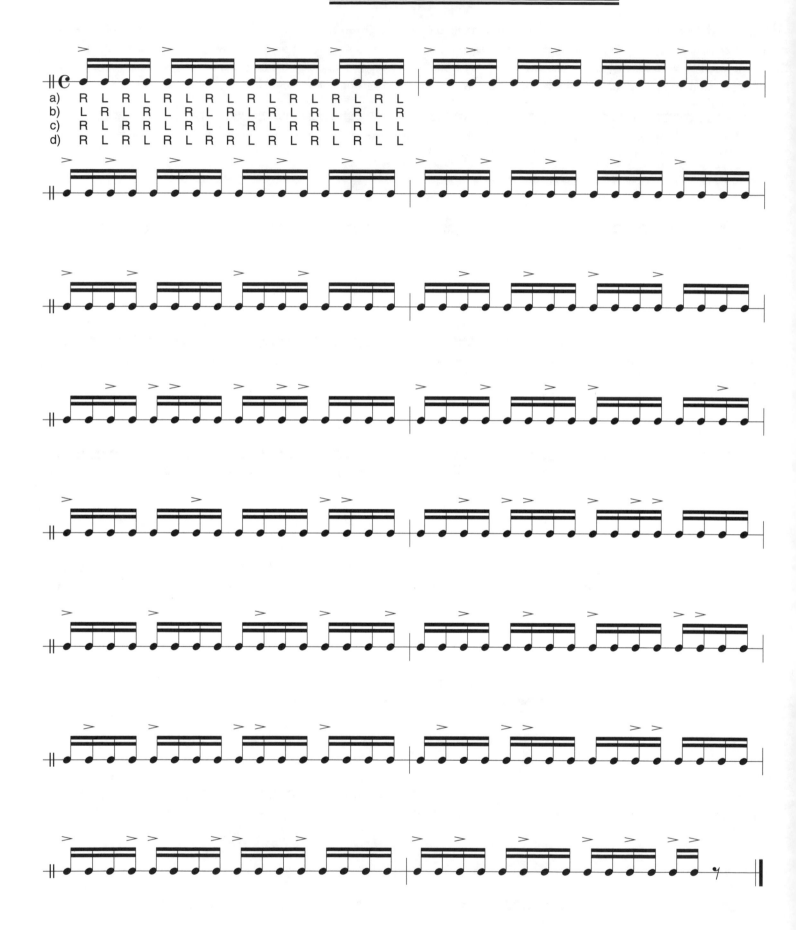

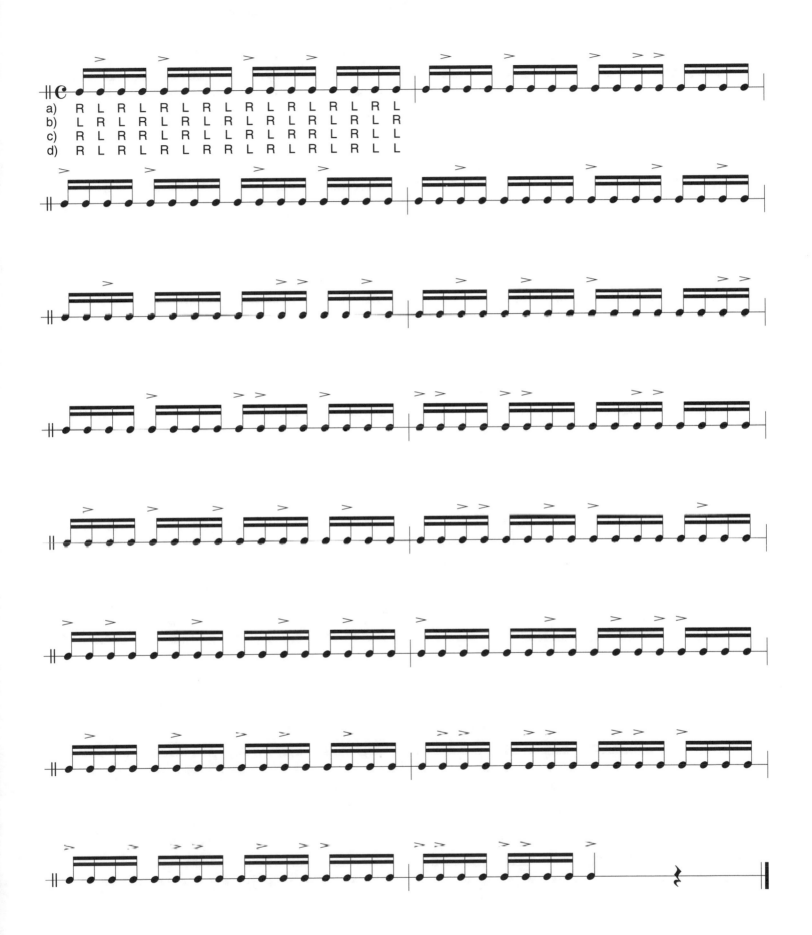

a) R L R L R L R L R L R L R L R L
b) L R L R L R L R L R L R L R L R
c) R L R R L L R R L L R R L L R R
d) R L R L R L R R L R L R L L R L

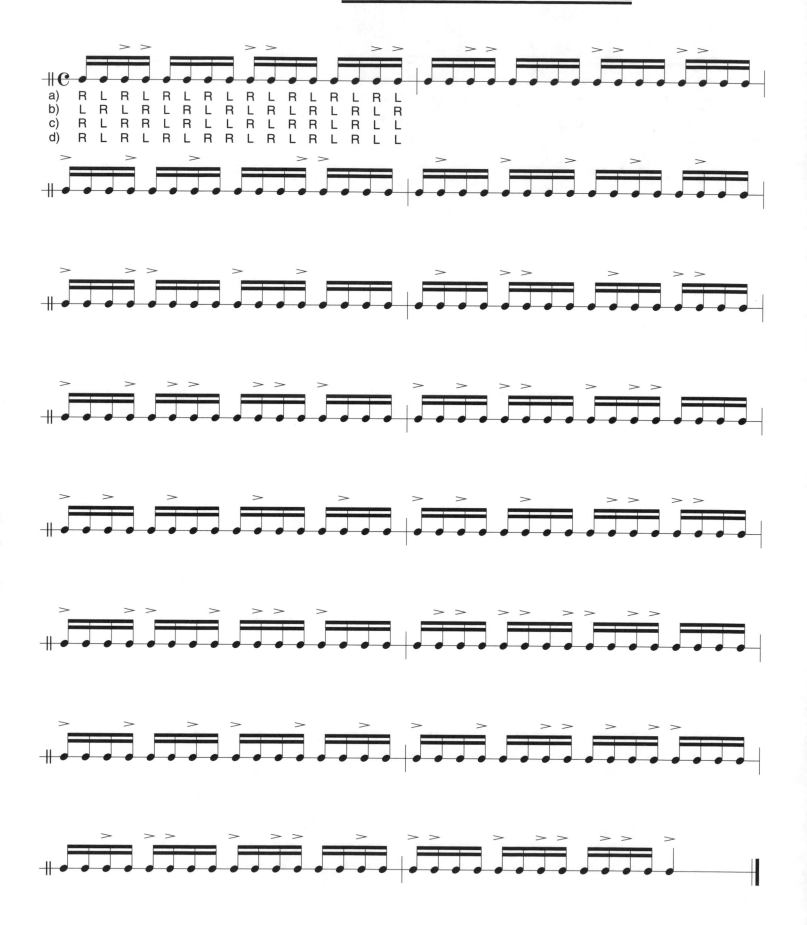

The following sticking patterns apply to the first measure:

a) R L R L R L R L R L R L R L R L
b) L R L R L R L R L R L R L R L R
c) R L R R L R L L R L R R L R L L
d) R L R L R L R R L R L R L R L L

ONE-BAR ROLL PATTERNS

All of the following 16th-note roll exercises should be played using a closed buzz roll. Be sure to play all accented notes much stronger than the unaccented notes. Remember to practice leading with both hands, and with the bass drum on all accented notes as shown below.

1
a) R L R L R L R L R L R L R L R L
b) L R L R L R L R L R L R L R L R

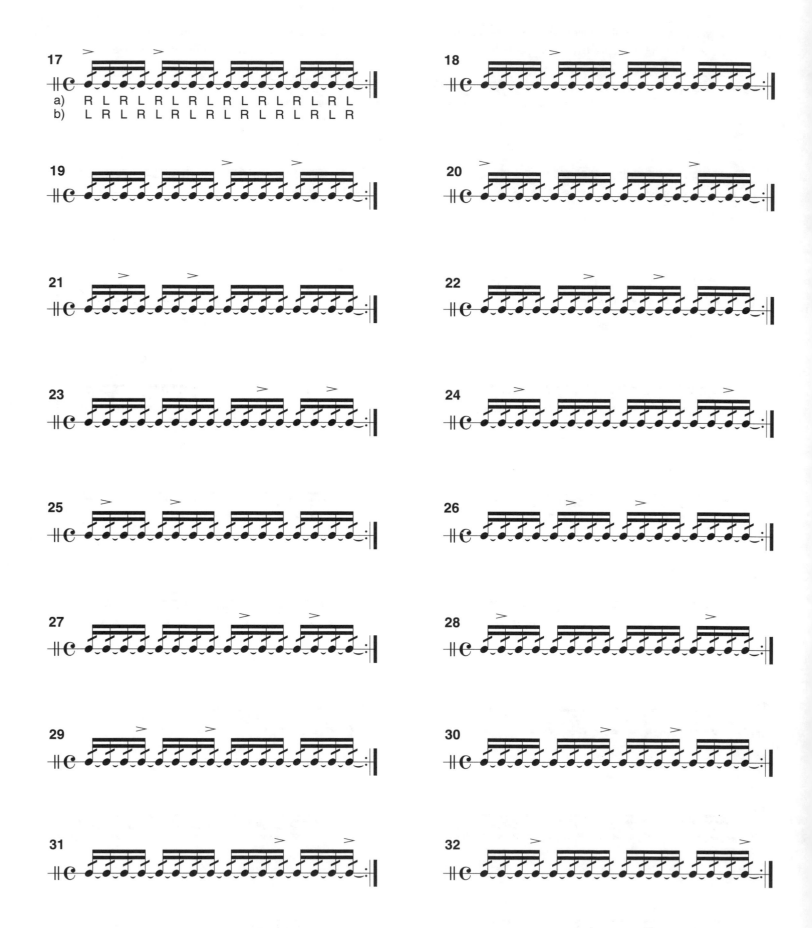

17
a) R L R L R L R L R L R L R L R L
b) L R L R L R L R L R L R L R L R

18

19

20

21

22

23

24

25

26

27

28

29

30

31

32

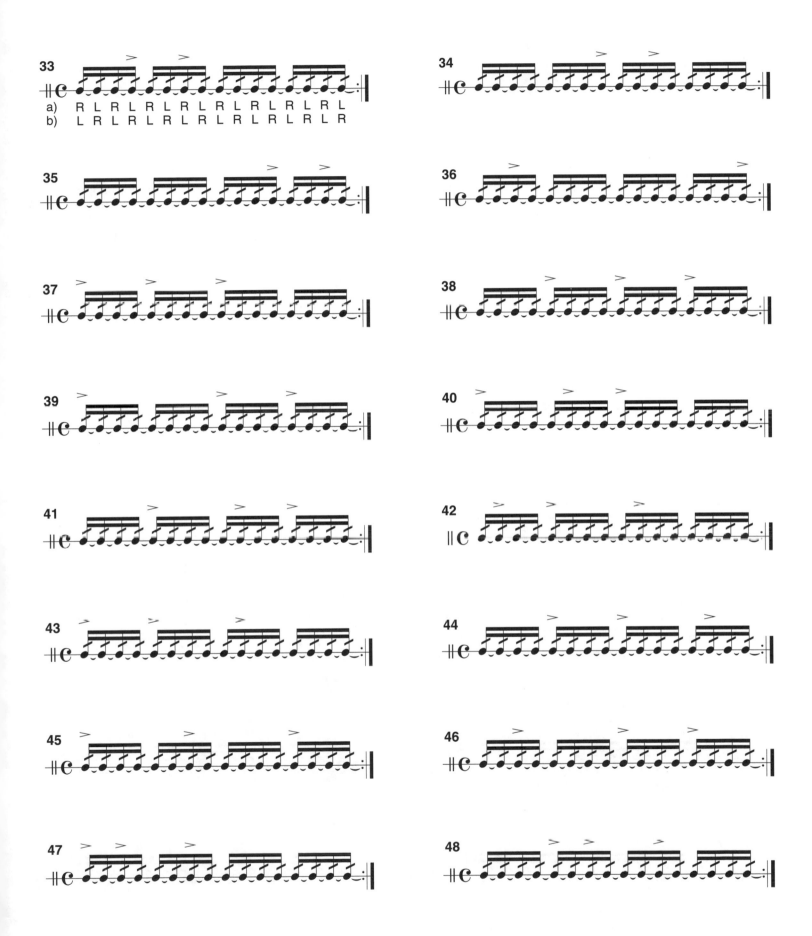

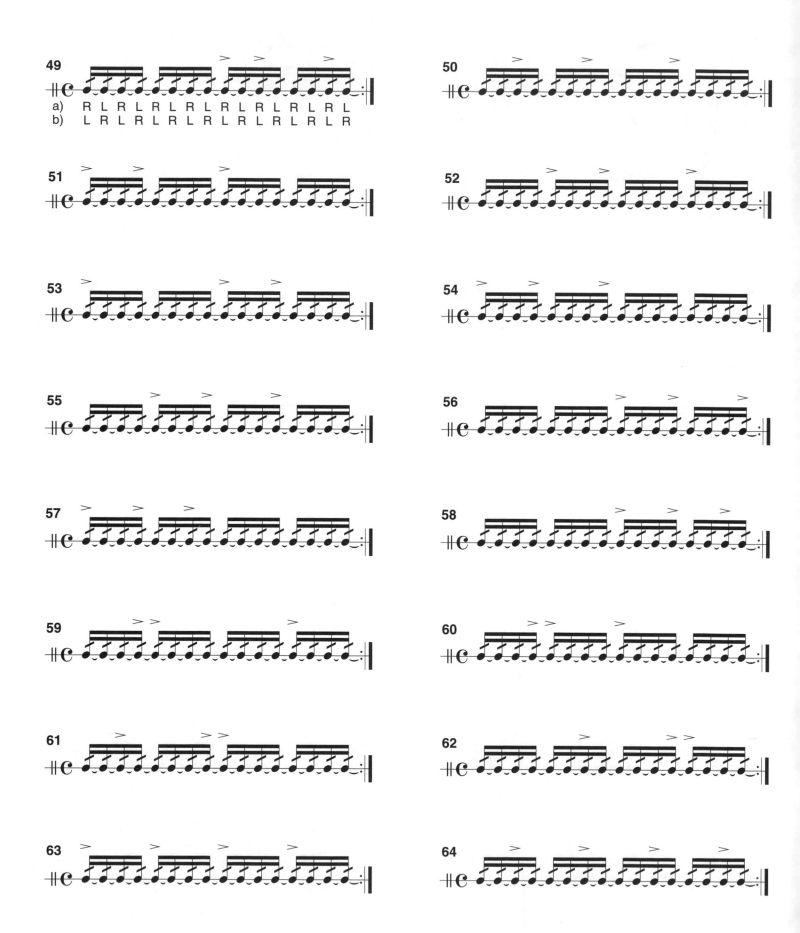

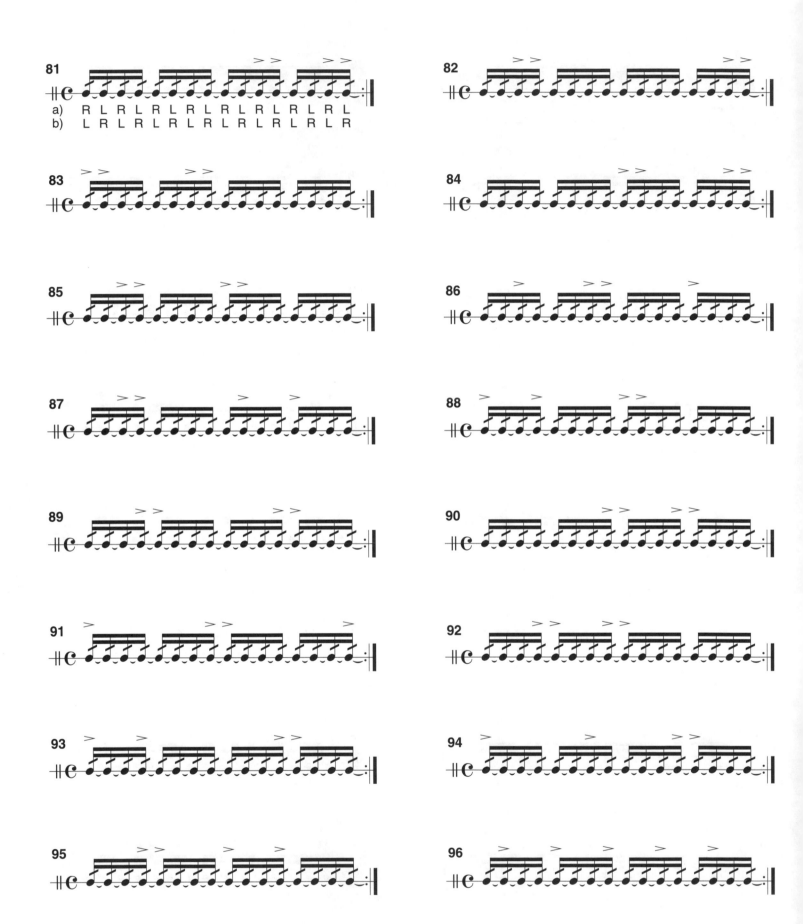

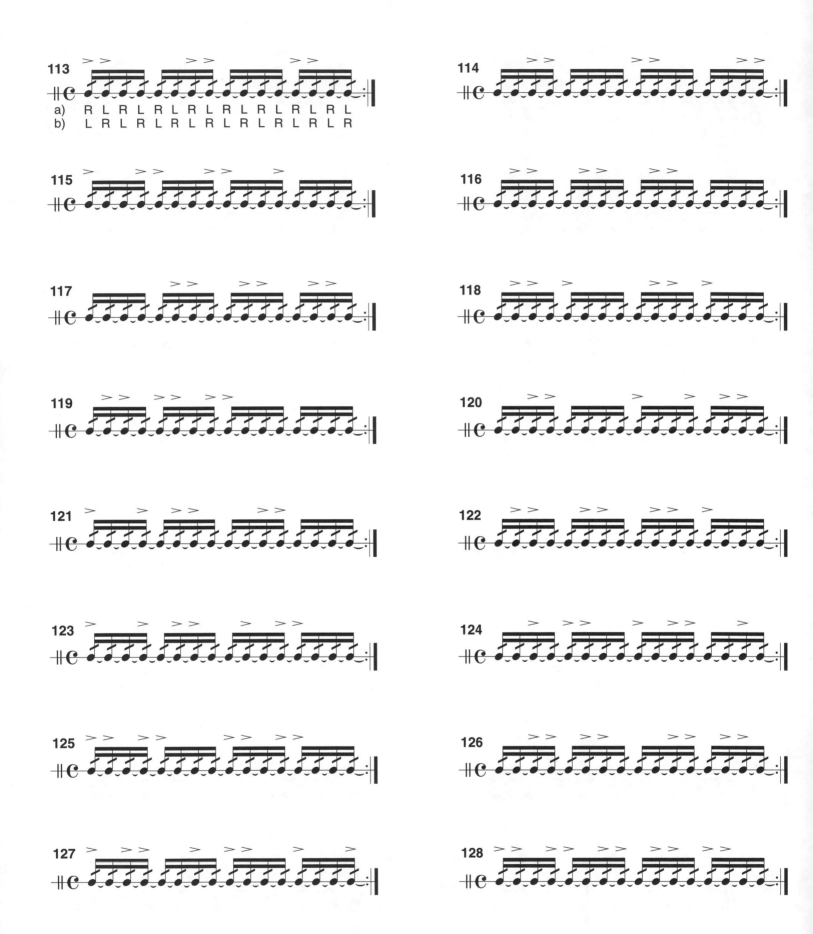

TWO-BAR ROLL PATTERNS

Take your time with these two-bar roll exercises. Increase speed gradually as your facility improves.

1

a) R L R L R L R L R L R L R L R L
b) L R L R L R L R L R L R L R L R

2

3

4

5

6

7 
a) R L R L R L R L R L R L R L R L
b) L R L R L R L R L R L R L R L R

8

9

10

11

12

13

a) R L R L R L R L R L R L R L R L
b) L R L R L R L R L R L R L R L R

14

15

16

17

18

Practice each of these four-bar patterns at least five times before proceeding. Be sure to practice leading with each hand (stickings a and b).

1

a) R L R L R L R L R L R L R L R L
b) L R L R L R L R L R L R L R L R

2

3

4

a) R L R L R L R L R L R L R L R L
b) L R L R L R L R L R L R L R L R

5

6

7

a) R L R L R L R L R L R L R L R L
b) L R L R L R L R L R L R L R L R

8

9

16TH-NOTE ROLL SOLO #1

This sixteen-bar, 16th-note roll solo, and the three that follow, use many of the previously studied 16th-note accent patterns. Practice leading both with right and left hands, and then add the bass drum on all accented notes. Start slowly and increase speed gradually.

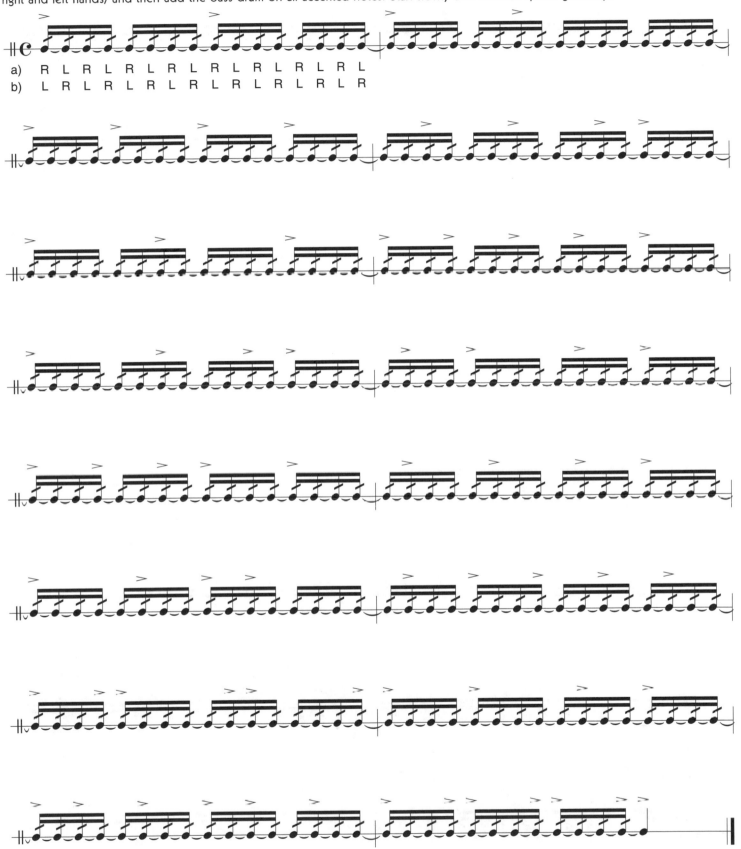

a) R L R L R L R L R L R L R L R L
b) L R L R L R L R L R L R L R L R

a) R L R L R L R L R L R L R L R L
b) L R L R L R L R L R L R L R L R

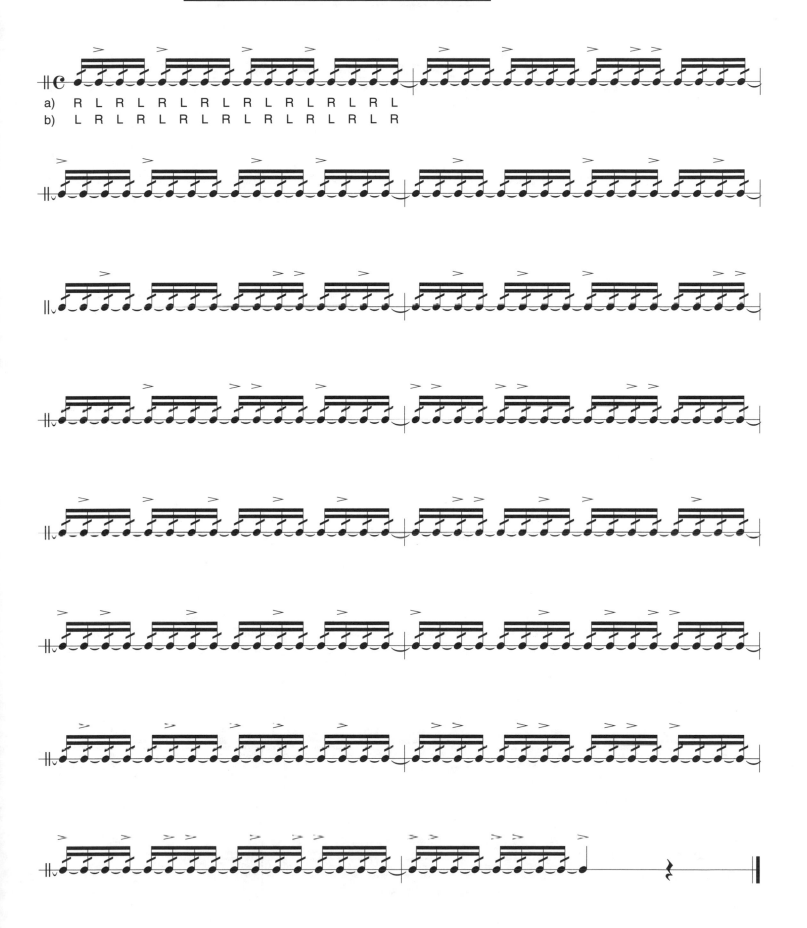

a) R L R L R L R L R L R L R L R L
b) L R L R L R L R L R L R L R L R

a) R L R L R L R L R L R L R L R L
b) L R L R L R L R L R L R L R L R

From Today's Hot Young Players...

...**Danny Carey** (Tool), **Taylor Hawkins** (Foo Fighters), **Ginger Fish** (Marilyn Manson), **Kevin Miller** (Fuel), **Tyler Stewart** (Barenaked Ladies), **Tré Cool** (Green Day), **Stefanie Eulinburg** (Kid Rock), **Tommy Stewart** (Godsmack), **Al 3** (Powerman 5000), **Dave Buckner** (Papa Roach), **Tony Fagenson** (Eve 6), **Paul Doucette** (Matchbox 20), **Samantha Maloney** (Hole/Mötley Crüe), **Jon Fishman** (Phish), **Abe Cunningham** (Deftones), **Greg Eklund** (Everclear), **sPaG** (Mudvayne)...

...To The Legends Of Drumming...

...**Charlie Watts, Jim Keltner, Tito Puente, Steve Smith, Hal Blaine, Manu Katche, Glen Velez, Terry Bozzio, Peter Erskine, Will Kennedy, Jeff Hamilton, Simon Phillips, Richie Hayward, Roy Haynes, Zakir Hussain, Omar Hakim, Airto, Rod Morgenstein, Mel Lewis, Ricky Lawson, Billy Cobham, and more.**

Young Drummers And Old. Hot New Players To Seasoned Veterans.

MODERN DRUMMER COVERS IT ALL!

Subcribe today! Mail the coupon below, or

subcribe online at www.moderndrummer.com

THE MODERN DRUMMER LIBRARY

Master Studies
by Joe Morello

The book on hand development and drumstick control. *Master Studies* focuses on important aspects of drumming technique.
06631474 • $12.95

The Great American Drums
by Harry Cangany

The history of American drum manufacturing. A valuable collector's reference source.
06620010 • $19.95

The Drummer's Studio Survival Guide
by Mark Parsons

The definitive book on recording drums, for the novice to professional drummer.
00330257 • $12.95

The Drummer's Time
by Rick Mattingly

A compilation of enlightening conversations with the great drummers of jazz, from Louie Bellson to Tony Williams.
00330454 • $12.95

The Modern Snare Drummer
by Ron Spagnardi

38 exciting solos for the intermediate to advanced snare drummer that challenge both reading and technical skills. Perfect for percussion majors and as audition and contest pieces.
00330458 • $12.95

The Encyclopedia of Double Bass Drumming
by Bobby Rondinelli & Michael Lauren

Designed to improve your double bass playing ability, this progressive book focuses on developing a comprehensive double bass drum or double pedal drumming style. Incorporates a variety of styles including rock, funk, and blues.
06620037 • $12.95

Applied Rhythms 06630365 • $8.95	**Great Jazz Drummers** 06621755 • $19.95	**The New Breed** 06631619 • $12.95
Best of Concepts 06621766 • $9.95	**Electronic Drummer** 06631500 • $9.95	**The Working Drummer** 00330264 • $14.95
Best of Modern Drummer: Rock 06621759 • $9.95	**Progressive Independence** 00330290 • $12.95	**Cross-Sticking Studies** 00330377 • $12.95
When in Doubt, Roll 06630298 • $13.95	**Drum Wisdom** 06630510 • $7.95	

* Prices, contents and availability are subject to change without notice.

FOR MORE INFORMATION, SEE YOUR LOCAL MUSIC DEALER,
OR WRITE TO:

HAL•LEONARD®
CORPORATION

7777 W. BLUEMOUND RD. P.O. BOX 13819 MILWAUKEE, WI 53213
WWW.HALLEONARD.COM

0401